Praise for

God in the Alley

"Greg Paul tells stories of whores and crazies, misfits and rejects, that sound as if they stepped out from the pages of the Bible. The only difference is that he finds them on the streets of Toronto instead of the Jericho road and at the Samaritan well. But they continue to be Jesus stories, every one—honest, accurate Jesus stories of which he gets to be a part."

—EUGENE PETERSON, professor emeritus of spiritual
theology, Regent College, and author of numerous books

"I dare you. No, I double dare you to read this book at more than one sitting. Each page is a seat belt that straps you in, and the turning of the page pulls the straps tighter. When the ride is over, you'll want to start again."

—LEONARD SWEET, author of numerous books including
Out of the Question...Into the Mystery

"Greg Paul has been my guide on several encounters with the street people of Toronto. To him they are not 'the homeless' but rather his friends; he knows them by name, is familiar with their stories, and treats them with a mixture of respect, sensitivity, and concern. I think the reader of this moving narrative of Greg's work at Sanctuary will be hard pressed to decide whether he finds God in the back alleys of Toronto or takes God in there with him."

—HON. HILARY M. WESTON, former lieutenant governor
of Ontario (1997–2002)

"Through Greg Paul's eyes, we're surprised to see Jesus here and now—alive and right in front of us. He doesn't preach at them: 'I have learned too well the bitter emptiness of chirpy gospel-talk to ones so deeply wounded.' Instead, he listens to them. He shows up and gets to know them. He sets aside his plans enough so that God has space to act. And Jesus moves in Greg's heart and in his actions. And now in his writing, that light also shines. I am grateful to have read this book."

—DAVID WILCOX, musician, songwriter, and storyteller

"With the writing of this book, Greg has not only told his story and the story of those who live on the periphery, but he has called us, his readers, to come to grips with our own prejudices and brokenness and to understand what it means to follow a suffering Savior."

—DR. ROD WILSON, president of Regent College, Vancouver, British Columbia

"A riveting book. From the first story in this book, you are drawn into a world that Jesus walks in and through."

—MARSHA MARKS, author of *If I Ignore It, It Will Go Away…and Other Lies I Thought Were True*

"We should have known better: all our elaborate and contrived efforts to discover Jesus in our midst, and all the while the kingdom has been among us, though hidden beneath its tumble-down exterior. What's more, the King himself is here, only wearing the disguise of the least of these. With candor, humor, and love, Greg

Paul tells his tales of urchins and vagabonds, streetwalkers and panhandlers, and in doing so pulls scales from our eyes to reveal Christ for us, with us, in us, through us. The experience of reading this book haunts, convicts, delights. But one thing is for sure: You don't want to miss it."

—MARK BUCHANAN, author of *The Holy Wild: Trusting God in Everything*

"Greg Paul has found the courage—and the calling—to walk as Jesus walked among the disillusioned, the downtrodden, and the discouraged. Read *God in the Alley* and you will be encouraged to look for lonely people where you live."

—ANGELA HUNT, author of *The Debt*

"Profound yet simply and poetically written, *God in the Alley* is engaging, inspiring, demanding, and so needed. Greg Paul writes with a poetic eye for detail and a deep love and affection for those whose lives have intersected with his. Detailing his own journey in learning to live a life of compassion and grace, he inspires and invites us all to join him in the journey of living the life of Christ, every day and every hour of our own lives."

—DEVLIN DONALDSON, author of *Pinocchio Nation*

God in the Alley

BEING AND SEEING JESUS
IN A BROKEN WORLD

GREG PAUL

SHAW BOOKS

an imprint of WATERBROOK PRESS

God in the Alley
A SHAW BOOK
PUBLISHED BY WATERBROOK PRESS
2375 Telstar Drive, Suite 160
Colorado Springs, CO 80920
A division of Random House, Inc.

All Scripture quotations, unless otherwise indicated, are taken from the *Holy Bible, New International Version*®. NIV®. Copyright © 1973, 1978, 1984 by International Bible Society. Used by permission of Zondervan Publishing House. All rights reserved. Scripture quotations marked (KJV) are taken from the *King James Version*. Scripture quotations marked (NASB) are taken from the *New American Standard Bible*®. © Copyright The Lockman Foundation 1960, 1962, 1963, 1968, 1971, 1972, 1973, 1975, 1977, 1995. Used by permission. (www.Lockman.org).

Details in some anecdotes and stories have been changed to protect the identities of the persons involved.

ISBN 0-87788-092-1

The prologue, "Neil's Story," appeared in a slightly different version in *Moved with Compassion,* ed. Brian Seim, copyright © 2000 World Vision, published by Essence Publishing.

SHAW BOOKS and its aspen leaf logo are trademarks of WaterBrook Press, a division of Random House, Inc.

Library of Congress Cataloging-in-Publication Data
Paul, Greg, 1958–
    God in the alley : being and seeing Jesus in a broken world / Greg Paul.
        p. cm.
    Includes bibliographical references and index.
    ISBN 0-87788-092-1
    1. Paul, Greg, 1958– 2. Sanctuary (Mission : Toronto, Ont.) 3. Rescue missions (Church work)—Ontario—Toronto. I. Title.
        BV2657.P28A3 2004
        277.13'541083—dc22
                                                            2004011319

Printed in the United States of America
2005

10 9 8 7 6 5 4 3

To everyone mentioned
(accurately named or otherwise!)
within these pages.

What a journey we're on together!

Contents

Acknowledgments

I don't suppose any book has ever been written that was truly the product of one person. This one, I think, owes its existence to even more people than most.

My wife, Karen, has been my partner on this journey from the beginning, through some challenging and very costly experiences, and was one of the voices that made it clear to me that it was time to write this stuff down. Mike Clarke, Jeremy Horne, and Heather Ann Lowry spoke similar words, and at a time when the notion of being able to actually take the time to write seemed patently absurd. The rest of the staff at Sanctuary affirmed the importance of doing so, and, in fact, held me to account for doing it. Their partnership in ministry, along with that of my brothers in Red Rain, has meant, and continues to mean, more than I can briefly express.

Sue Mosteller of L'Arche Daybreak, Kent Annan, and Karen Stiller offered critical editorial input before I submitted the manuscript anywhere, and did so in a way that was profoundly encouraging. Sue and Maureen Wright of the Henri Nouwen Centre also offered practical support in a couple of other ways that were as surprising as they were generous.

Henri Nouwen's friendship and his writing, as well as the work and writing of Jean Vanier, have provided a framework for understanding and valuing the concept of brokenness that is at the very core of this book—and at the core of my own journey as a disciple of Jesus.

Don Pape, Rita Dotson, and Elisa Stanford at Shaw Books have been more encouraging, and more sensitive to my peculiar concerns about the manuscript, than I could ever have hoped. I think I have accepted virtually all of Elisa's editorial suggestions with hardly a quibble.

Tim Huff, Phyllis Novak, Dion Oxford, Joe Elkerton, and a handful of people from Yonge Street Mission, including Rick Tobias, Dave Adcock, Matthew Parker, and Bill Ryan, to mention ony a few, have been friends and partners in ministry here on the streets of Toronto for years. They have taught me and inspired me by their long-term commitment to the poorest of the poor.

My kids—Caleb, Jesse, Rachel, and Kelly—hold me tight, challenge me, and bless me every day. They also frequently teach and inspire me by the freedom with which they accept and even love those who are ignored or rejected.

But this book belongs most of all to the people whose stories are told within. They're my companions, my friends, my teachers. With gratitude for being invited to share the journey with them, I dedicate this book to them.

Finding Sanctuary

T hat stretch of Queen Street in Toronto's West End was the place
hookers went when they became too old, addicted, or ill to with-
stand the competition and brighter lights of the downtown core. It
was afflicted with a rash of dollar stores, thrift shops, and the kind
of tiny diner that has four mismatched tables, a selection of second-
hand kitchen chairs, and a six-item menu, printed in magic marker,
on a sheet of cardboard tacked to the wall. When the provincial government emptied the nearby nuthouse in the seventies—"reintro-
ducing psychiatric patients into society"—the residents, with no
structure or support, drifted along Queen Street like industrial waste
pumped into a nearby river. Used up, disregarded, and tossed out.

On one corner, some optimist had engaged in a small-scale
redevelopment, trying to bring suburban culture to the inner city
in the form of one of those L-shaped, single-story, brick-and-plate
glass strip malls. Two of the six stores were abandoned already. A
Laundromat and convenience store remained along with West Side
Johnny's, a roadhouse bar that had expanded into two of the original spaces.

Four men piled out of a big, old, brown Chevy van in front of

West Side Johnny's, opened its doors, and began unloading musical gear onto the sidewalk. Two of the men grabbed a bass amp and began lugging it into the bar. The bar itself was straight ahead; to its left were a dozen steel table-and-chair units bolted to the floor, sparsely populated with old guys in ball caps drinking Blue and watching the big-screen TV sports report. Still wrestling the amp through the doorway, one of the musicians glanced to the right. A single pool table stood isolated from the surrounding gloom beneath an overhead light. He heard a grunt and a muffled shout, then two shadows lurched into view in front of the table. They were perfectly backlit, as one shadow raised a cue and broke it smartly over the other's head.

The musician sighed. *Here we go,* he thought. He gave a moment's consideration to picking the amp up and hauling it straight back to the van. He glanced at his companion. Their eyes met for a moment. Then they shrugged, picked up the amp, and carried it in past the bar without a word.

It was the early nineties, as the hometown Toronto Blue Jays were rolling toward their first of two consecutive World Series championships (the band watched Dave Winfield stroke a game-winning home run that night on the big screen, while they tried to keep the groove alive), and the band's name was Red Rain. But the story starts much earlier than that...

◆

As in many inner-city churches of a certain age, the original sanctuary had been added to, built around, and finally relegated to hosting odd events peripheral to general congregational life. The members of Danforth Baptist Church, in the heart of Toronto's Greektown, met on Sundays now in a much larger and more formal sanctuary replete with oak pews and soaring windows. They'd been doing that so long that nobody thought of it as the new sanctuary anymore and hadn't for years.

The old sanctuary was a vacant cube with the tall pebbled-glass doors of other smaller rooms staring into it. The rooms had once been Sunday-school classrooms; now one was the church office, and the others collected the detritus of a half-dozen different groups borrowing space. The walls were hospital green, faded and water-damaged and smudged into a dull kind of camouflage—as if undecided about offering healing to wounded souls or going out to do battle for them. Ten feet up the high walls, cast-iron hot-water radiators floated, as if pausing a moment before ascending on up to glory. The wooden floors were bare, dark at the perimeter and worn pale toward the center of the room. A low plywood platform, painted flat black, squatted at one end. A scattering of folding two-set chairs provided clues as to how the room had last been used and by whom: a few drawn together in a corner for an impromptu prayer meeting or Bible study; four or five rows near the stage for a recital offered by the students of the piano teacher who lurked in the basement. A big open space with the chairs shoved helter-skelter to the perimeter meant dancers.

The first time I walked into that room, in February 1985, three musicians were sitting on or near the stage, leaning on their instruments and chatting quietly. I had backed up John Palmer for several years, but he was the only one of the group I knew. He introduced me to the drummer, Les Brown (balding, bushy-bearded, with a skinny "rat tail" of hair hanging down his back), and Dan Robins, a guitar player with a Dylanesque mass of curls. Under my arm I carried a Roland EP-10, possibly the cheesiest electric piano ever made. I set up, and we jammed for a while.

It was a curious mix. Les had spent years as the only white member of a large, black, Pentecostal reggae band. Dan was definitely a rocker, and John and I had spent most of our time as an acoustic duo, playing the folky songs he'd written. We lurched from one style to another, and the fact that we had no bass player didn't help the strange combination. The music wasn't very satisfying, but there was an intriguing intensity about these men. After we had butchered a half-dozen tunes, Les deliberately put down his sticks, ran a hand over his head, and pinned me with a faintly aggressive stare.

"So," he said. Pause. "What are you doing here?"

I was a little taken aback. I was there at John's invitation and knew that these guys were talking about forming a band. At twenty-six I was the youngest one there—it was clear they were past just playing for fun or for the sake of coolness. Still, I really had no clue what Les was on about.

"Well," I said, looking down at the can of soda I had picked up. "I just came for the free pop."

Actually, I had no sense of what was about to unfold in my life. Although I'd dabbled in songwriting since my teens, I considered myself (still do) to be a mediocre piano player. I had been backing up Johnny because he was a friend and because I believed Christians needed to reclaim the arts as a medium for the expression of their faith. My own passion was for writing fiction, and I had received enough encouragement to think I was on the right track. Furthermore, I had a wife (Karen), a toddler, and another child on the way. I was working full time as a carpenter in a booming construction market.

All of us had been doing the Christian coffeehouse circuit in and around Toronto for a number of years. Dan and Les had come together out of a spiritual compulsion to do something different—they kept talking about "taking it to the streets." At the time, none of us knew quite what that phrase meant.

I found the group intriguing and inspiring, but Karen and I agreed that it most likely wasn't for me. After attending a few more practices, Karen and I prayed about it halfheartedly. I met with the guys twice more, expecting each time that it would be my last. I had no desire to get in the way of what seemed to be God's direction for them. Karen and I were seriously considering moving north to the bush country near Lake Nippissing, with the goal of eventually helping establish a retreat community for Christian artists and thinkers. To our surprise, God answered our prayers clearly and definitively, by the miraculous provision of a much-needed keyboard. It seemed clear that his direction was for me to put aside the fiction writing and the dream of a log cabin in the woods and embrace this—the band and the city—as my calling.

Within weeks we had been joined by Sean O'Leary, a bass player with a mass of wild blond hair, a fretless Gibson, and a brand-new passion for Jesus. That spring, a handful of people who were planning to open a new Christian coffeehouse came to listen to us practice. The coffeehouse would be called The Trojan Horse, and fittingly, its purpose would be preevangelism. As we understood it, that meant surreptitiously softening people up so they'd be ready (eventually) to hear the good news. After they audited four or five of our songs, we drew together a few chairs and sat down to listen to them explain, with some embarrassment, that our material was "too overt" for their purposes. This statement was a portent of things to come. We would hear similar words through the years, but strangely, always from Christians and never—not once!—from the managers and patrons of the many bars where we would end up performing.

We went through a number of changes over the next few years. First Sean, and then John, moved on. Dan in particular recognized what I wouldn't: that I should be the frontman for the group and the lead singer, instead of staying comfortably in the background. There were several other important members of the group through the years (I hope they'll forgive me if I don't list them), but the lineup solidified in the summer of 1994 when we were joined by Doug Virgin and his vintage Fender Jazz bass. The lineup is the same today. The Jazz, alas, has moved on.

By the fall of 1990, we'd had to move out of the old sanctuary at Danforth Baptist and through a succession of other practice facilities. Eventually, the small and mostly elderly congregation of Central Gospel Hall, near Yonge and Bloor, welcomed the band to use their building as a place to meet, pray, and practice. When we met spiritually interested people in the bars and coffeehouses where we played, we often invited them back to Central to jam or talk. Sometimes they came because they wanted to *pray* with us— a radical and vaguely dangerous notion for them.

As this ministry developed, Karen and I became convinced God was revealing to us the nature of the calling we had been trying to discern for years. Early in 1991, we approached the elders of Richvale Bible Chapel about it, and in March 1992, the church commended us to full-time ministry—and boldly commissioned me to play rock'n'roll in bars for Jesus!

From that seed grew a community of faith in the downtown core of Toronto known as Sanctuary. A few others were involved at the time—notably Alan and Colleen Beattie, Les's wife, Sherry, and Kate Jones—and still others have arrived since, drawn by a sense of God's calling to come and share their lives with his precious poor. The Beatties, married only a year or so, were the first to move from suburbia to the city to answer that call, and again others followed, including our family. In December of 1992, the old Central Gospel Hall congregation packed it in, passed the torch to us, and dispersed, leaving us with their blessing and a hundred-year heritage of living out the gospel in the inner city. The name Sanctuary went on the building the following spring. We bought the place in December 2000—a tale of miracles in itself.

The actual worshiping community is only, at this writing, a small body of about forty people. It includes people who live "normal" middle-class lives in most respects, and others who are or have been street-involved: homeless, addicted to various substances, involved in the sex trade, and so on. A small but highly dedicated staff, and the larger group of volunteers they direct, regularly reach out to our broader community of about four hundred street-involved or at-risk people. Most of these are not people who would describe themselves as followers of Jesus, yet many would call themselves members of the Sanctuary community. The stories that follow are theirs.

In a phrase, I have shot these scenes in soft focus. While the reader should know that I have been very free with some details, in the most fundamental way, these stories are true. I have obscured identities and simplified story lines a little, and I have definitely not told the *whole* truth. The background experiences of my friends are, in every case, more painful and more extreme than I have dared to relate here. I have told only what I felt was necessary to properly convey the essential truth of each story. Nothing central to the stories has been manufactured.

Where possible, the owners of these stories have read and approved them—often with tears in their eyes over old pains and new joys. I have tried especially hard to make certain that only the person or persons involved (or friends who know them intimately) would know for sure precisely who the stories are about. The one exception is Neil's story. It is as accurate as I know how to make it.

I have come to have a deep admiration for the courage, humor, tenacity, surprising grace, and incredible capacity to endure that I see every day in my friends from the street. Many of them have fought battles for decades—from the time they were children!— that would have exhausted all my mental and emotional resources in months. Society in general tends to dismiss them as losers. I have come to see them, battered and broken as they are, as tragic heroes.

Still greater heroes are the ones who have had the courage to leave those dependencies behind and step out, eager but terrified, longing for something they've never known, looking for Jesus.

Prologue: Neil's Story

I remember sitting on Neil's steeply pitched roof, wearing cowboy boots and a leather jacket, scooping leaves and mulch out of his eaves trough and into a garbage bag by my side. And I remember very clearly asking myself, *What am I doing here?* It wasn't just the absurdity of risking life and limb to clean someone else's gutters while my own remained full, or the unnerving way my boots slipped on the wet shingles that made me ask that question. It was the sense that I had intended to be something much bigger than Neil's free maintenance man. In my own heart, I had come to be the presence of Christ to him, and I was having a hard time seeing where my current activity fit.

Our relationship began as one contracted by the AIDS Committee of Toronto (ACT), of which I was a volunteer, and Neil a client. He had come to ACT seeking a practical assistant, a kind of buddy and gofer. I had come to ACT seeking a way to engage the gay and lesbian community—Toronto has one of the largest gay and lesbian communities in the world, and Sanctuary is located in a corner of it. I knew that as a Christian; a straight, married father of four; and an evangelical pastor, I would look very much like the enemy to people who had been shunned and even driven out of the church. Often, this rejection happens while gay or lesbian people are still young and still struggling with their sexual and spiritual identities. And, not infrequently, they simply slink away from the church, convinced that it is not a safe place in which to admit their struggles. I knew that I would look and sound like one of the people who, in truth or perception, had presented a callous and judgmental face to gays and lesbians when they most needed loving acceptance and Christian nurture and admonition. In truth, I *am* one. I came to the conclusion that I needed to be in a place where I would have to submit to the direction of gay and lesbian people, where I would be accountable to them for my attitudes and actions, and could learn something of their culture. In short, I would try to be *among* them, instead of trying to reach them from outside. In fact, I needed to move away from thinking about "them," and learn to think about "us."

It seemed to me that this was what being the presence of Christ was all about. After all, Jesus came to be among us, and he put himself in a position of ultimate submission to us, even allowing us to take his life. He came among the poor, not the rich; dwelt with the weak, not the powerful; made himself of no reputation rather than seeking the famous. And he lived and died in submission to our rules and regulations, while never being subverted by them. Since ACT was, at that time, largely an organization of and for gay and lesbian people, it seemed a logical place for me to learn how to be a "safe" person to that community.

After completing ACT's volunteer training and a number of

short assignments in the fall and early winter of 1993, I was given Neil's name and address in the new year. I spent the winter shoveling his walk, taking out the garbage, sometimes doing a little grocery shopping, and, in early spring, clearing his eaves troughs. For the first four or five months, the relationship I hoped for seemed to be going nowhere. It began to irk me that Neil, who was so well-off financially—he'd been employed in international banking—was so good at accessing free support. He had Meals on Wheels, a housekeeper a couple of times each week, one or two other connections, and me. All volunteer services and all for which he could have afforded to pay the going rate.

In time I began to realize that, despite the seemingly constant flow of service providers through his Cabbagetown home, Neil was a terribly isolated man. Few of the people moving in and out of his environment offered anything substantial in the way of relationship. For the most part, the service providers were just that: professionally compassionate and professionally detached. It was hard to imagine, but I wondered if Neil perhaps preferred it that way. Every time I visited Neil, I would pause outside the gate from the lane into his backyard and pray for the opportunity to talk about Jesus with him. I would also promise God not to speak until such opportunity clearly presented itself; I have learned the hard way that, when zeal overwhelms wisdom, tenderness, and humility, people run. Apart from describing my work as a pastor to hurting and needy people in the downtown core (some of whom bought drugs or worked as prostitutes just a few streets away from his house), the opportunities to share more of myself and Christ seemed restricted, both in frequency and in scope. Neil kept me at a distance, just as he did other service providers.

In late spring I began to sense that Neil, like me, was hoping for something more from our relationship. It occurred to me that perhaps he felt he had no right to look for anything more than a provision of some simple services, given that it was a contracted and prescribed association. One sunny day, as we weeded his garden together ("Neil, is this a weed or a plant?" I had to ask repeatedly), I pushed myself abruptly off my knees and back onto my heels. Neil paused and looked at me.

"Neil," I said, "I know I'm just supposed to help you out with odd jobs, but something tells me you'd rather have a friend. If that's what you want, I'd rather be a friend."

I intended to go on and tell him that, if he really just wanted a helper, I was fine with that, too. But I never got it out, because he spoke immediately and quietly. "I'd like that very much."

That was all for then, but our relationship slowly began to change. He was more content to just sit and talk, and we began to look for things to do together just for fun, instead of chores that needed doing. I still did some shopping and various odds and ends around the house, but we also went to an art gallery, a park, an arboretum, and even an automotive show when he felt well enough. But by the time the fall auto show rolled around, Neil was in a wheelchair and on oxygen. He talked about buying a silver Caddy, never acknowledging that he could no longer drive. "A little denial is good for you," he used to say with a wry grin. But he did observe more than once that there wasn't much point in his trying to save money any longer.

Later that fall, somebody broke into his house while Neil was home. Neil had heard him working at the door, trying to get in, but was paralyzed by fear. He had been in the washroom anyway, and he simply locked the door and sat as quietly as he could on the toilet while the burglar stole his stereo and fled through the backyard and into the alley behind. The experience left Neil badly shaken. He called to tell me about it, describing how frightened and vulnerable he had felt. His own house no longer felt safe to him.

"Could you come and bless my house?" he asked. "Is there some kind of ceremony you can do?"

Neil had been raised Mormon, but coming out as a gay man had meant excommunication. He never completely ditched Mormonism, though—he just added an incredible mix of other religions and philosophies on top of it. As somebody said at his funeral, "Neil had an eclectic faith." Having spent my life in Brethren churches, where terms like *ceremony, ritual,* and *liturgy* sound like words of a foreign language, I had no idea what Neil was hoping for.

"Sure," I said. "When do you want me to come?"

I took a Christian friend to whom I had introduced Neil before, and who was, himself, HIV positive. The three of us walked slowly throughout Neil's house, stopping in each doorway and praying aloud for God's protection on the house, and for the reality of his presence to be made very real and comforting to Neil.

Neil beamed, and his sense of relief and restored security was palpable. From that day on, he asked me to pray for him often.

Through early winter, his health continued to deteriorate. At Christmastime, wheelchair-bound and dependent on oxygen, he flew south to visit family in North Carolina. Within days of his return, he landed in the hospital. When I went to see him, he was a little disoriented, peevish, frightened, and even more shockingly emaciated. For the first time, I found myself wondering how long he had left. He recovered enough to be sent home with overnight nursing care, a daily housekeeper, and a couple of other kinds of support.

One morning a couple of weeks later, I was driving by his street around ten o'clock when I felt impelled to drop in on him. Just for ten minutes, I told myself. As usual, letting myself through his back gate, I prayed for the opportunity to talk to him about Jesus. Then I went in and read the note the nurse had left on the kitchen counter. There was nothing unusual, and the nurse had signed out at seven that morning. I climbed the stairs to his room.

The room was hot, humid, and ripe as a mushroom factory. The cat was curled up on the windowsill, looking disdainful. And Neil was writhing in a soundless panic in the bed, half sitting up, his pajama bottoms and the bed sheets wound around his ankles, his spindly arms flailing in a futile effort to free himself, a look of sheer terror on his face. He had soiled himself, and it was everywhere. He was disoriented, uncertain where he was or what was happening to him.

As I spoke quietly to him, freeing his limbs and stripping the soiled sheets from the bed, he calmed down. I ran a tub full of hot water, removed his pajamas and carried him to it. While he soaked, I went back to the room and cleaned it up. The soiled bedclothes went to the basement laundry and fresh sheets went on the bed. I went back to the bathroom and helped him out of the tub onto a chair, where he could sit and dry himself. I brought fresh pajamas, and dressed him. Then I carried him back to his bed. He seemed almost weightless, just bones shrink-wrapped with grayish skin. His temples were hollow, and his teeth seemed too large for his face.

By this time, he was thoroughly exhausted. He lay quietly back against the pillows and allowed me to take his feet, one at a time, and tuck them under the covers. Doing so, I noticed that one foot, somehow, had not gotten completely clean. Getting a washcloth, I wiped that foot. As I did so, I was struck by what I can only describe as a powerful revelation, two streams of thought converging, and both seeming to me to be the voice of God.

Cradling his foot in my hands, my mind was filled with the image of Jesus washing the feet of his disciples at the Last Supper, a towel around his waist, determinedly taking the servant's role. I had been meditating on that story from John's gospel just the day before, and now I could almost see Jesus hunched over Peter's foot, his hair hanging forward and obscuring his face, quietly insisting against Peter's protestations that those feet, but only the feet, needed to be washed. *This moment was what my whole time with Neil had been for! This was what it meant to be the presence of Christ.* I had been looking for opportunities to preach, wanting to effect a clear and possibly dramatic conversion. I realized in that moment that my longing for those things was as much or more an indication of my desire to be successful as they were of my passion for Neil's soul. It became clear that, being Jesus to Neil, while it certainly included praying for him and announcing the good news to him, was most perfectly summed up by the mundane and even odious task of gently wiping excrement from his foot.

At the same time, I was deeply touched by his profound vulnerability. His foot was bare, and he hadn't even enough strength left in his ruined body to lift it and put it back under the covers. The words of Jesus were ringing in my ears: "I needed clothes, and you clothed me, I was sick and you looked after me…. Whatever you did for one of the least of these brothers of mine, you did for me."[1] This, too, was the purpose of my time with Neil. For the first time during our whole relationship, I saw Jesus in Neil. I had been seeing him as someone upon whom I could practice my own imitation of Christ, and had missed the Presence right before me. *I recognized that Neil was, at that moment, a physical representation to me of a vulnerable and dying Christ.* Jesus was allowing me to clothe him, and look after him, by caring for his "brother."

After a quiet moment or two, trying to assimilate these powerful impressions, I asked Neil if he would like to pray. "Yes, I'd like that," he whispered. I prayed first. I have no idea what I said. When I was done, I thought Neil might have fallen asleep. But then he spoke, whispered, into the stillness of that room. He didn't address his prayer to anyone, just spoke. And the words he spoke were words of blessing upon me. He knew he was dying, yet he asked nothing for himself; instead, he blessed me! Then he was so quiet and still, I thought again that he might have drifted off. But he spoke once more, without opening his eyes, and his voice this time was clear and surprisingly strong.

"In the name of Jesus."

Apart from saying good-bye, they were the last words I ever heard him speak. When I visited him again a couple of days later, he was curled up in a tight little ball, unconscious. A week after that, he was gone.

By inviting me to walk with him to his death, Neil gave me a great gift, perhaps the greatest gift that anyone can bestow on another. In a sense, he gave me his life, by allowing me into some of his most vulnerable places at what certainly must have been the most vulnerable time he ever knew. And God took his gift and multiplied it, introducing me through the experience with Neil to a new and fuller way to live the gospel.

Although I have characterized this event as a revelation, I have to say that I am still learning this new way, and I have a great distance to go—some stretches of the journey I seem to traverse over and over. I enjoy the fact that Jesus called himself "The Way," and that the early disciples were referred to as "belonging to The Way." It reminds me that this way, although it is in some respects new to me, is really very old, and a great many others have walked it. More importantly, it reminds me that the journey is as important as the destination. In fact, it could be said that the journey *is* the destination, for the journey itself is Jesus himself. This way leads me toward my truest home, the place where I'm learning to reside in Jesus; this way also leads me away from my old self, a place where bitterness and brokenness obscure my true identity, and toward the Cross. Here, at this *crux,* this meeting place, that self that is plagued and crippled by sin dies. A new, true self is resurrected, and the reality of Jesus in me unfolds.

The glimpse I received during that pivotal experience with Neil of what it means to be the presence of Jesus to another person, and what it's like to see Jesus's presence in others, was brief and bright as the lightning-strike illumination of a darkened landscape. There have been other lightning strikes before and since, some nearer and longer, others faint, fleeting, and distant. I'm learning to cultivate an illuminating awareness, an ability to hold that fleeting image in my mind after it's gone, to *behold* it. There are times when the whole landscape seems less dark, as if the dawn were approaching. That's what I want this book to be about: the cultivation of our ability to both be Jesus and see Jesus, if only by a dim flickering light—the afterimage on the darkened retina of a momentary, brilliant burst.

One essential lesson I learned from Neil was that recognizing Jesus's presence is just as important as being his presence to other people. I find that, often, I am like the two disciples who were on their way to Emmaus after Jesus had died. They didn't realize it was the resurrected Jesus who had walked along with them until he had left them again![2] It's often after the fact, when I take time to pray and meditate, that I recognize Jesus, either as he has been present to me, or as he has been present through me. The more I learn about these things, the clearer it becomes that truly being Jesus and truly seeing him cannot be separated. In fact, the two are interdependent. As truth becomes something other than truth without love, and vice versa, I cannot recognize where Christ is present and the Holy Spirit is at work unless I am willing to be truly present as Jesus to someone, with all the personal investment and vulnerability that implies. Think of what it cost Jesus to be present with me! Neither can I hope to truly be his presence, whether proclaiming the good news, modeling his love, or standing for truth, unless I recognize that he is already there and active—that he got there ahead of me—and I open myself in humility to behold him. My capacity to be the presence of Christ in the world is dependent upon my willingness to see his presence also.

On this journey, then, this journey deeper into the land of Jesus, I can be guided by these two beacons, being and seeing. Steering exclusively for one or the other will take me off course; I'll end up traveling the wrong path, and I'll miss my destination— and both the path and destination are Jesus himself. Jesus is also the guide, the pioneer of my salvation, and so I am on this journey as a follower, or disciple. If I seek to act as a member of the body of Christ, his proxy physical presence in the world, and eagerly seek him as the one who has promised to be "in the midst," I am submitting myself to a course of spiritual discipline. A discipline is what is required of disciples: a deliberate choice, or series of choices, to follow and emulate the Master.

Hockey players lift weights. Boxers skip rope. Downhill skiers ride bicycles. Coaches devise patterns and programs to hone very specific abilities that, when put together, will make the athlete a more complete competitor. The competitive athlete may be strong, fast, and skilled, but it is the coach who calls the shots. The athlete who won't submit to the coach is a fool. Paul's several uses of sports imagery in his letters remind me that becoming what God has called me to be requires similar submission, energy, dedication, and intentionality.

The disciplines involved in being and seeing Jesus are also forms of spiritual cross-training. The practice of one sharpens the ability to "perform" the other. When I speak of disciplines, though, I don't mean exercises that are performed diligently each day for a short time. I mean the regular, intentional cultivation of an attitude, an awareness such as Paul wrote about in his letter to the Philippians: "Let this mind be in you which was also in Christ Jesus..."[3] If I am going to emulate and follow the Master, I need to watch him, listen to him, walk with him, saturate myself with him. Reading and understanding the Bible is, of course, critically important, but it's not enough. Jesus must be allowed to invade my whole life. I need to learn to wear him like a coat, carry him consciously in my heart, and look for him everywhere.

Henri Nouwen described spiritual discipline like this:

In the spiritual life, the word discipline means "the effort to create some space in which God can act." Discipline means to prevent everything in your life from being filled up. Discipline means that somewhere you're not occupied, and certainly not preoccupied. In the spiritual life, discipline means to create that space in which something can happen that you hadn't planned or counted on.[4]

Being Jesus is a discipline of action. If I truly want to be present as Jesus was and is, I must choose to act in very specific ways. Theory, or doctrinal correctness, is not enough. Seeing Jesus is a discipline of stillness. If I really want to see him, I'll need to avoid being consumed by trying always to do things in his name, and I'll need to learn to be motionless, intent on beholding what is in front of me. These two disciplines are often in tension with each other; it's difficult to be still and active at the same time. But they strengthen different sets of spiritual muscles, and each discipline ultimately benefits the other.

Being Jesus requires that I choose to be actively present. Seeing him means that, paradoxically, in my being present, I must choose the stillness of being hidden—that is, rather than being focused on what I am doing, and seeking attention for it, I must be actively looking to see how Jesus is presenting himself in and through others. Being present the way Jesus was means that I have to abandon my own power. And seeing him in others teaches me the power of abandonment. Being Jesus is a call to give my life, as he himself indicated when he called us to pick up our crosses. But seeing Jesus opens me up to a new way to live, to a resurrected life. The wonderful gift God gave me through Neil was that moment of revelation—and the continued, growing realization—that being and seeing Jesus are intrinsically connected. In fact, they're often happening at the same time.

Being Present

Choosing to be present doesn't sound like much of a discipline. It seems like it should be an easy choice to make, and a simple thing to do, but I'm coming to realize that it's neither. When I take a good look at myself, I see how much trouble I often have really being there in different situations. When one of my friends is a few minutes into a drunken shaggy-dog story, my mind skips tracks and heads off in a different direction. Some of my friends have serious psychiatric problems, and when one begins to tell me about the latest visit from angels or his latest victimization by a conspiracy of police forces across Canada, or that he's a secret agent for a chain of coffee shops, I find myself laughing or moaning inside, taking a mental step back. Even at home, the safest place I know, the same kind of thing happens. Every now and then, I do valiant battle against my tendency to sink myself into my work, and I triumphantly carve out a little more time to spend at home. And every now and then, I wake up with a start to the fact that I have an amazing capacity to be home but *absent*...my nose in a book or a newspaper, even my Bible...fiddling with some private project, functionally absent from the people who mean the most to me.

Truly being present, and more especially being present as an emissary of the Christ, definitely requires a deliberate choice, sustained by disciplined action.

It seems to me that the incredible story of Immanuel—"God with us!"—rests on one statement containing two simple but profound concepts: God *sent* his Son to be *among* us. My capacity to be the presence of Jesus will require of me that I be *sent* to my world and that I learn to be *among* the people I find there.

God is sending me out of the little world I have constructed around me, where everything that reassures me is within easy reach and I am at the center of it all. Being sent from a comfortable, supportive environment—middle-class Christian family and church —into a street culture of violence, poverty, drugs, and prostitution is at first unnerving. Gradually, though, even these dynamics become normalized. I discover a new challenge: to be sent, not just to the streets, but beyond the internal barriers I have erected to protect myself.

◇

March is a wicked, sneaky month in Toronto. The sun sneaks from behind the clouds to lift your heart for an hour or so, then the clouds—mean, colorless—come rushing in to cut off the light and drizzle slush all over streets still bordered with dirt and cigarette filters, the detritus of departed snow. At night the wind whistles in off the lake, rushes up Yonge Street, and spreads out through the alleys and down the side streets like the wake of a motorboat, and almost as wet. Joe Abbey-Colborne is my street-work partner, and on this night, with midnight and all sense of natural optimism long gone, we are trudging past Maple Leaf Gardens along Carlton Street.

So this ancient, drunken gnome comes rolling out of the Coffee Time and tilts himself along the sidewalk toward us, the bottom half of a Styrofoam cup clutched in one grubby claw. His route is less than direct, but he's clearly navigating with us in his sights. He has a cancerous-looking toque mashed on the back of his head, the thick, round-shouldered look of the multilayered, and rubber boots with one flapping sole. He heaves to a stop in front of us, waving the cup in our general direction.

"Spare some change fer somethin' to eat?" he croaks. Looking more closely at him, I realize he's not quite so troll-like as I had thought. Despite a ratty plaid shirt, and a baggy, loose-knit sweater that could have been just about any color originally, there's a surprising noble quality to his features, and the hair and beard that had looked like a nest for small critters now seems, suddenly, more like a mane. He has one of those magnificent wedge-shaped noses, meant for leaning into the wind. It's clean and straight, hardly a broken capillary in sight. His eyes are blue and clear, and they seem to look just a little past us. He could be a Viking, or a Scottish chieftain.

I don't even take my hands out of my pockets. "Just gave away all my change, boss. Sorry." Joe looks closely at him, then roots around and comes up with a few small coins. Rob Roy doesn't even look at them, just jingles them absently in his cup, looking thoughtful. He's younger than I thought, somewhere between thirty-five and fifty. The scarcity of the coins Joe has bestowed upon him seems not to matter; in fact, I get the distinct impression that he asked for money purely out of habit, and that he's not even seeing it as he stares into his cup. Suddenly, he leans toward me, tilts his bushy head to one side, and squints up at me like a bad caricature of a marooned pirate.

"Are you afraid t'die?" His voice is like the grinding of truck gears, but he is not mocking or threatening, just asking.

He wants an answer, and the first thought that flashes through my mind is *I'm not getting sucked into this.* I am not interested in engaging a morbid drunk in philosophical or theological debate, on the sidewalk, on a blustery night, while working girls sail by like gaudily painted galleons under full canvas. I have learned too well the bitter emptiness of chirpy gospel-talk to ones so deeply wounded. The briefest thought of the incredible investment it would take to communicate a whisper of the truth and beauty of grace, the miraculous healing required to open those ears, that heart, to the possibility of forgiveness, the miles he would have to be carried before he could see, in the distance, the borders of the land where love dwells—these thoughts pass like a javelin through my mind, leaving me weary and a little cranky. I am profoundly *bugged* by my inability to offer anything to this man that he might realistically grasp. I want to protect myself from the sense of futility that will hang like a mist in the space he vacates after I "witness" to him and he slopes off down the street to his next bottle of Listerine. I want to say nothing; I want to back up, go in another direction. But he's still standing there, and he still wants a response.

"Afraid to die? Yeah, I guess so. I think everybody's at least a little afraid of it."

He nods, once. "I'm afraid t'die. I'm afraid t'meet Jesus." So blunt, so serious, but matter-of-fact, as if he was saying, "I'm afraid it might be cold tomorrow." I'm pretty sure he's not setting me up because he's made me out as a religious type. I've never seen him before, and in my usual garb I'm more often identified as a drug dealer or an undercover cop than a minister.

But it seems so obvious and natural that, almost without thinking, I respond: "Really? That's about the only part of it I'm *not* afraid of." (And immediately to myself: *Oh boy. You just got suckered into this.*)

He goes on as if he hasn't heard. "I'm afraid to meet Jesus because I don't got an answer."

"Oh, that's easy, man! The answer is, he loves you!" I can't believe I'm saying this. I wonder again if I'm being set up. I definitely don't want to go there. But what else could I say? And him— you'd think I'd just thrown him a lifeline. He cocks an eye at me, bright and hard as a marble, from beneath an eyebrow like a shrub.

"D'ya think?" he says sharply, his whole body suddenly tense and expectant as a diver on the high board. Well, yeah, I'm trying to say, but he has thrown an arm around my neck and drawn my face into his hair and beard in a strong and fervent one-armed embrace; the other hand still holds his cup. I'm surprised to realize that there is not a whiff of alcohol on him; he actually smells *clean*. My mouth is next to his ear. How can I not speak?

"Jesus loves you, man. So much—he died for you to prove it.

You don't need to be afraid." His arm tightens even more for a moment, then he releases me entirely. Stepping back, he shakes hands with both of us, solemn as a penguin, then he smiles, spins away, and tumbles off along the sidewalk. Joe and I are watching him go, a little stunned by the unexpectedness of it. Part of me is still waiting for him to experience a miracle conversion, followed quickly by a request for five bucks.

He is perhaps fifteen or twenty yards away when he stops, tilts his head back and laughs, a hearty, happy laugh, big enough to hang in the air despite the nasty wind whipping along Carlton Street. Now he is *sauntering* away, and I find myself elated, wondering who's been witnessing to whom.

"There are angels everywhere," I say to Joe as we cross the street.

Being sent may be enough to guarantee my own presence, but it doesn't necessarily follow that I will *be* the presence of Jesus, too. For this, I need to learn how to truly be among the people to whom I am sent, as Jesus was among us. The character of my presence needs to be like his. I am sometimes struck by thoughts of the hundreds of lepers Jesus did not heal, the thousands of people who died of ridiculous little infections during his lifetime, the blind or lame beggars who missed his passing by a few hundred yards or a few minutes. He healed so few! And I, who can heal no one, am reminded that being his presence does not mean fixing everything.

Being among people means being in their midst, not outside.

It means being with them, not being over them. It means not looking away from their agony or humiliation, but beholding it, and having the courage to be also wounded by their pain.

Samuel was an Ojibway man in his twenties who, despite years of substance abuse and street life, carried himself with grace and dignity, even when under the influence. One day, as we talked about the terrible, constant anger that seethes inside of him, I asked if he could identify when it started, or where it came from. He was a little bit stoned, and his stream-of-consciousness description of the scene made it even more harrowing. He never told me how it came about, or who did what, but he just painted a lurid picture of himself as a young child, watching his mother die beside him, while his father, drunk and howling, raged like a storm around him. From others who have worked with him, I have learned that Samuel was subsequently fostered by a white Christian family, and that he was physically and sexually abused by the father while in their "care." His life on the street for more than ten years had been the usual litany of disaster, pain, and self-destruction. Incredibly, he had not turned his back on Christ or Christians, although he struggled constantly with both.

On the first Sunday of the new year, Samuel joined us for the "Sunday thing." He sat beside a young Christian woman who was a member of our worshiping community and who had known him for many years. As usual, we started with singing some songs of praise. If I'm not mistaken, Samuel requested one of the songs.

And he definitely prayed. After others had offered more conventional praise and worship, during one of those quiet moments, he spoke into the still air: "Thank you for keeping me alive... I'm just glad to be still alive."

I knew they weren't idle words. I knew Samuel had lost streetmates to suicide, overdose, accident, and even murder, and that he had survived physical, sexual, and substance abuse, street and family violence, and plain old killing cold.

Each Sunday, when we celebrate the Lord's Supper together, we explain what the bread and the cup represent and point out that, among other things, partaking of them constitutes a public statement that the individual believes that Jesus is Savior, Lord, and the Son of the living God. We encourage people to be honest with God and themselves about what they do and do not believe. "If you don't believe it," we say, "don't fake it. Don't take the bread or the cup just because the person next to you does. Feel free to turn it down if you're not sure what you believe." As it happened that Sunday, I gave thanks for the bread and passed it around. When I offered it to Samuel, he waved his arm at me in a broad, angry gesture of dismissal. When we had finished sharing this simple, powerful symbol of the almighty God's decision to come among us and give himself for us, we spent a few moments in quiet contemplation of the cup—his blood poured out for our forgiveness and cleansing.

In the midst of that quietness, Samuel exploded. He leapt to his feet, yelling, arms flailing, staggering, covering his face momentarily with his hands. "You don't know who I really am...don't know!...Lord, have mercy, have mercy...mercy on me..." He stumbled around for a few seconds, banging into chairs and bumping into a few people who had leapt up in alarm. Finally, he staggered out, moaning, accompanied by the young woman who had been sitting beside him. A few seconds later, I followed them outside.

It was painful to watch. Samuel was facing into a corner of the building, moaning and muttering, reaching out every few seconds to touch the wall with a hand already bloodied from punching the bricks. It struck me that he looked like a devout Jew wailing at the Western Wall in Jerusalem, touching the wall, bowing his head, then raising his face to the sky as if pleading with God. The young woman stood behind him, touching his arm gently and making soothing noises. Samuel poured out his despair in wave after wave of mutters, moans, and body-shaking sobs. Tears streamed down his face, and although I remember few of his words, I know he told of overwhelming loneliness, hopelessness, shame. He told of betrayal and abandonment. He told no stories, didn't rail against the government, his family, whites, or anybody else for that matter. He simply unloaded his heart, a deep, deep well of emotional and spiritual agony. "Too much peace in there," he said at one point, waving toward the room where, presumably, the others were by now sharing the cup. He touched his chest: "No peace here."

Two other men joined us, both recovering addicts. The young woman still stood patiently at Samuel's elbow, speaking quietly to him now and then. He responded gently to her, but then lifted his head and moaned again, "You don't know who I am..." One of the men jumped in: "I *do* know, man. I know what it's like. I was addicted to heroin for many years, but now I'm free of it. You could be too." The other man made similar noises, but Samuel just shook his head wearily, still with his back to us, and made a gesture of dismissal with his hand. He reached out his other hand and leaned briefly against the wall. "You don't know who I am," he repeated softly. It seemed to me that he was telling us that it wasn't substance abuse that was the issue, but his own bleeding soul. As I think of him now, the words of Isaiah come to mind: "The whole head is sick, and the whole heart is faint. From the sole of the foot even to the head, there is nothing sound in it, only bruises, welts, and raw wounds, not pressed out or bandaged, nor softened with oil."[1]

Whether because I couldn't stand the sound and sight of his pain anymore, or because, as usual, I felt like I had to say *something,* I leaned close and spoke in his ear. I called him by name and, weeping a little myself, told him how precious he was. Made in the image of God. Worth dying for. For the first time, he turned his head toward me and regarded me through streaming eyes. "I respect that," he said simply, then turned away again. But it didn't seem to comfort him much. The rawness of his pain seemed to radiate from him, and I felt it like an assault on my own heart. The ache was only increased by the recognition that I had nothing— nothing!—but my presence to offer.

After a few minutes, I left him, but the young woman stayed, as the women had stayed at the foot of the cross, saying little, but sharing Jesus's pain. Over the two or three days that followed, I tried to figure out why this event had affected me so deeply. The rawness of Samuel's pain was hard to witness, of course, but that certainly wasn't a new experience for me, and it didn't explain the curious sense of excitement that seemed to hover around me, then scoot away whenever I turned my head to look at it straight on. Slowly, it sorted itself out in my mind. As it was for the two on the road to Emmaus, the breaking of the bread was the clue.

When I began to think about the fact that Samuel's pain exploded between the breaking of bread and the sharing of the cup, other things began into fall in place. Now, I'm *not* saying that Samuel was a literal epiphany. But I do believe that God, in his gracious and redemptive way, spoke to us through Samuel's pain and gave us a graphic portrayal of his Son's rejection, abuse, pain, and loneliness, even his sense of having been abandoned by the Father. He reminded us that he knows what our pain is like—he's been there. And he reminded us of our great hope, since he took on flesh and blood so that, through his own death, he might destroy the one who holds the power of death—that is, the devil— and deliver those who through fear of death were subject to slavery all their lives.[2] Even Samuel.

❖

I could only receive this precious gift of the revelation of the presence of Christ through Samuel by being truly with him, vulnerable to being wounded by the outpouring of his pain—by being the presence of Christ to him myself. Trying to fix him would only have kept the reality of the situation at arm's length, with zero chance of my actually helping him. He showed me how hard it can be to look the suffering Christ in the face and not walk away. It was hard to watch, hard not to view his explosion merely as an interruption of the decorum of our worship. It was hard not to see him as someone "other," one from whom I was separate and distant. It would have been easy, once Samuel had run outside, to view the matter as over and simply return to the "real" business of praise.

This kind of active, fully engaged presence requires tremendous discipline. In the Sanctuary community, the challenge is to find ways to be with addicts, alcoholics, homeless people; people who regard sex as a sport, business, or weapon; atheists and anti-Christians; and devotees of Wicca, animism, Buddhism, and a variety of other faith systems. The challenge is essentially the same in the worlds of business, education, or government. How do I practice this presence among people who are, much of the time, engaged in activities in which I can't—don't want to!—participate? When I think of trying to be the presence of Christ in this fashion, it no longer seems benign and faintly condescending. Instead, it seems risky, uncomfortable, humbling. Giving some money to a panhandler is something I know I can manage; it can even make me feel good about myself. But embracing him as a brother, literally putting my arms around his smelly, drunken, psychotic, and possibly bug-ridden person, grappling with the concept that he, too, is beloved of God, precious, and made in his image—well, this provides an unnerving peek into my own soul. It can be even worse if I discover that panhandler is sane, sober, and clean.

I am not at all sure that I want to recognize the ways in which we are alike. Choosing to be among the addicts and panhandlers of our neighborhood doesn't require that I go live under a bridge or begin drinking mouthwash. We are alike in many ways more fundamental than a few self-destructive habits. We are broken, fatally flawed—and immeasurably precious, made in God's image. Jesus's coming among us reminds us of both these things.

One cold February night several years ago, my wife, Karen, and my eldest son, Caleb, then eleven, were walking up Yonge Street. Looking across the street, they saw a man they knew who had been in drug rehab for several months. We had received word that he had left the program earlier that day, and there he was, drunk, sitting against the window of a Thai fast-food joint, panhandling. Crossing the street, they stood in front of him. If I'd been there, I would likely have been angry with him. Karen wept— "Oh, Derek!" Caleb simply bent down, put his arms around Derek, and told him he loved him. That's being present. And you can imagine what the people watching from inside the restaurant must have been thinking as they stood at the counter munching their spring rolls.

Seeing: Beholding the Hidden Jesus

H e had no beauty or majesty to attract us to him, nothing in his appearance that we should desire him."[1] These words of Isaiah have always intrigued me. More than any other passage of Scripture, they have left me wondering just what Jesus looked like: on the surface, apparently not very impressive. In fact, as Isaiah also says (and as I am learning from Samuel and others), "there were many who were appalled at him—his appearance was so disfigured."[2]

Jesus is as disguised or hidden today as he was when he walked the hills of Palestine. Trying to be truly present as he was present puts me in the place to see him—but to actually recognize him requires eyes of faith.

Behold is a word rarely used anymore, but it describes better than any other word what it takes to consistently recognize the face and voice of the Christ in my life. Most modern versions of the Bible use the much weaker word *look* instead. When John the Baptist said to his disciples, "Behold, the Lamb of God who takes away the sin of the world,"[3] he meant that they should do more than give him a cursory glance. To behold is to stare long and hard, to study visually, to drink in with the eyes—in fact, to *hold* that image in your mind after it is no longer in front of your eyes. I need to do precisely this when I look for Christ, expecting him to show up in surprising places, or I risk missing him entirely.

I often feel that Satan's greatest trick is just like the simple conjuror's misdirection: he keeps me looking to the right when Jesus is appearing to the left. Or I get so focused on being Jesus that I miss him when he's standing right in front of me. Most often, I think I miss him for one of three reasons: his *transcendence* (I miss his beauty soaring overhead while the grottiness of daily life consumes my attention), his *humanity* (he can seem so ordinary!), and his *brokenness* (the pain and disfigurement in which he is present is often appalling, and I recoil from it).

"There's no pain like the present!" Wendy said with a grin and her trademark toss of red curls. Mutt said nothing. They stood waiting in the parking lot, both of them shivering, hugging themselves, running shoes soaked through by the slush that is the predominant natural feature of Toronto in the winter.

Carlo's ancient gray Toyota came farting down the street, barely paused to admit them both, and turned the corner. A minute and a half later, the same car turned into the same parking lot. Wendy and Mutt popped out. Carlo took off, but they didn't wave or even give the departing car a glance. They were halfway down the alleyway behind the hotel before Carlo was out of sight.

Crack cocaine produces a rush as sharp and quick as the deal they had just made. Less than ten minutes later, they were scuttling back out of the alleyway.

The next day they were awakened by the strange combination of the heat of the sun on the blue construction tarp just overhead and the growth of a large frozen patch at the bottom of their sleeping bag. They clung to each other, pretending they were cozy. The regularity of cars swishing by on Rosedale Valley Road was hypnotic, but that frozen patch was getting hard to ignore. Finally, they scrambled out of the bag. Mutt pushed a couple of small puddles off the tarp and began searching among the cardboard, plastic, and blankets for clothing. Everything he found was dirty and cold. Some of it was actually frozen stiff. He paused while pulling on a second pair of track pants.

"Wendy," he said, "there must be more than this."

She looked at him to see if he was serious, then around the lean-to. She looked at the frozen sock in her hand, then back at him. She laughed a real belly laugh, the kind of laugh he loved her for even when she was laughing at him.

"You're a regular philosopher, Mutt."

It was the beginning of something, though. A day or two later, he took sixty dollars she'd made on a date and took her out to dinner. In a restaurant! They had steak and potatoes and no booze. They had coffee and desert—some "death by chocolate" kind of cake. Then they went to a movie, *City of Angels,* starring Nicolas Cage and Meg Ryan. A shamelessly mushy movie, and it was great. Wendy sniffled a bit at the end. They had pop and popcorn and

Glosettes Raisins, all of which they bought right there instead of smuggling them in. They didn't even sneak into another theatre to have a snooze through a second movie when the first was done. They got up, walked out through the lobby and onto the street, just like everybody else.

They bought Wendy a set of tights at a dollar store, which left them with less than a dollar. Then they strolled all the way down Rosedale Valley Road holding hands in the dark frosty night.

It was all so normal and beautiful that, as he stood outside the lean-to having a last smoke, Mutt thought his heart might explode.

Mutt had had his eye on Wendy for a couple of years before they actually got together. She'd been hanging with another guy— she always had a guy—a crackhead who didn't treat her right. One night, when her man was on the warpath, Mutt just grabbed ahold of her and walked her away. She had gone back to the crackhead once for a few days but returned to Mutt, and they had been together ever since. Four or five months now.

The beauty of that normal day put a hook into him. He felt like somebody was reeling him in, up out of the dark, weedy depths he'd been sliding around in for years, up toward the light and air. Up toward the thought that there was indeed something more. Of course, he'd always known that there was more to life than what he was currently living, just not for him. Until now...

He stopped using. Just stopped. He started hanging around more with the church people at Sanctuary, where Wendy had been taking him for drop-in meals. He started talking to God—out loud sometimes, saying—shouting!—"Jesus Jesus Jesus" when the jonesing got so bad he thought he'd lose it. Freaked Wendy right out. Her using tailed off too, although she'd still get lost once a week for a day or two, turn a few tricks, and smoke her brains out.

The thought of her out there running, doing one of her sugar daddies, laughing that wild laugh with whoever had an eight ball of crack…well, it was really starting to get to him. She'd come back exhausted and hollow-eyed and say nothing about what had happened. But he was always so relieved when she came crawling into the lean-to just before dawn that he could say nothing about it; he just took her in his arms and held her shivering self until she fell asleep.

Somewhere in there, it occurred to him that he loved her.

He'd been two months straight and sober (except for a little medicinal weed now and then) when he found a place they could rent. Just a tiny bachelor. Not even that, really: a room with a kitchen sink and hot plate and bar fridge in it, a little three-piece washroom, mottled turquoise walls and ceiling, and a map of Africa, rendered in mold, high in one corner. The kitchen sink blew bubbles when he flushed the toilet.

Even at that, they'd needed the church people to put up last month's rent for them. There had been a house-warming party, too, so they had some dishes, cleaning stuff, a futon, and some bed clothes. It was great. It was home, and Wendy was there with him. Just like normal people, like husband and wife.

For a week or two, it was bliss. A neighbor gave them a kitten. If Mutt woke in the night, he'd get up quietly, look out the window for a minute or two, then go sit on the toilet. He did all this slowly, luxuriously, conscious that he wasn't the least bit cold or damp. Sitting there, he would say quietly, "Thanks, God."

When the room got too small, they'd go out for a walk holding hands. Mostly, they avoided the corners where the action was, but every now and then they'd see a deal go down. They'd turn immediately, shivering suddenly, and hustle back to their room. They began to smoke a little more weed, trying to take the edge off the mounting restlessness. The room kept shrinking. Wendy worried some that she was gaining weight. It seemed that half the time, just touching her made her cranky.

One day Wendy said she was going down to the corner to get some smokes, and she didn't come back. By the time she was gone an hour, Mutt knew. He found her around midnight in a room on Pembroke. She was half-dressed, in the act of passing the pipe to the john she was with when Mutt booted the door open. The john took one look at Mutt, dropped the pipe, and vacated the premises. Mutt took a halfhearted swing at him as he ducked through the door.

"Why?" he screamed at her. "Why'd you go?"

She was stoned, looked like she'd been stoned for hours; she was a little freaky and absolutely flying, and she was gorgeous. She shrugged, unafraid.

"I dunno—I just needed to know if I still got it." She gave a little swing of her hips.

Suddenly, he didn't want to whack her anymore. And just as suddenly, he was huddling on the floor with her, sucking on the Coke can she'd been using as a pipe.

But it didn't do anything for him. He just felt empty, and kind of sick. He tried another zap, and it got worse. Mutt stopped then, but Wendy didn't, not till it was all gone. She passed out for a while, and they both slept until dawn. She followed him home then, but he could have been anybody leading her anywhere.

Their room seemed to shrink every time they returned to it—go down to the corner to get some smokes, come back five minutes later, and bing! the ceiling was magically a foot closer to the floor. It began to feel more like a cell than a room. Strangely, there were moments when this was comforting to Mutt. Sometimes he found himself pretending that they were locked in and couldn't go anywhere if they wanted to. Wendy didn't feel like that, though. She kept talking about going out, calling her sugar daddies. And, once or twice, she did.

Mutt started to go out and get into a little action of his own, just so he could bring some rock back with him, hoping she'd stay home. Hoping she'd love him a little again. Sometimes she did exactly that—loved him a little, with the emphasis on *little*. But increasingly, it seemed like she could hardly stand his touch. Couldn't stand him but was hot for almost anybody else. It was making him nuts. She'd smoke his crack, then go out anyway.

Now when she left she'd be gone for a couple of days. She'd come back snarling and unrepentant, sometimes even claiming he was so uptight it was making her go out. Friends at the church were telling him he had to let her go, stop chasing her into the crackhouses and trying to drag her home. Let her make her own choices. Pray. Realize that he couldn't save her or make her feel about him the way he felt about her. Mutt could see that this was true, but it just seemed impossible. What was he supposed to do, sit at home watching *Seinfeld* reruns on their cruddy old black-and-white while she was out there somewhere destroying herself?

They're right. I have to let her go, he'd say to himself a hundred times a day. And then, a moment later, returning like the ache of an old wound, a plaintive voice within: *But I love her...*

Mutt and I sat together many times over the course of a couple of years as he sobbed out the latest chapter in this story. They separated, Wendy finally opened herself up to Christ, and for a time, she actually did better than Mutt. They're both still on the journey, both still important members of the Sanctuary community and church, both still struggling in many ways—just like the rest of us. Lots of things about their lives and relationship have changed, but one thing at least has remained constant. Mutt still loves her, even if the character of that love has changed significantly.

When Mutt first began to tell me his story, it was painfully familiar. Still, I had the persistent feeling that it wasn't just the sordid tale of yet another codependent street relationship. Finally, it occurred to me that I hadn't just heard it before, I'd read it—in the Bible. It's the story of Hosea and Gomer, of course. Hosea was the Hebrew prophet who married a prostitute. Their relationship over many years was wracked by the kind of pain and difficulty you'd expect in a real-life story. There's no hint that they ever got to a point where they lived happily ever after. She betrayed him time after time, and even bore other men's children, but while Hosea let her go for a time, he never abandoned her. Their story became the story of God's incredible and stubborn love for his people.

The paradigm shift accompanying this realization allowed me to see Jesus yet again in the place where I least expected him. And it allowed me to value attitudes in Mutt and Wendy that I would otherwise have seen only as irritating, disappointing, or sad.

Mutt's love for Wendy was soaring, extravagant…and terribly unrealistic. Wendy was always ambivalent about her feelings for Mutt, while he was adamant that she was the "one." Mutt was far from guiltless in all of this. He was as thoroughly messed up as Wendy. He continually ignored the many signs small and great that this relationship was destructive for both of them. He believed his love could overcome her problems as well as his own. Frankly, the *transcendence* of Mutt's love for Wendy bugged me—and it was a powerful picture of the kind of Jesus love that covers a multitude of sins.

Just writing about Mutt and Wendy's relationship makes it seem more remarkable than it looked at the time. It was all so ordinary, so *human,* so much like the daily wear and tear that causes me to take my own wife for granted. So much like so many other relationships I've witnessed. And so much like Hosea, who spent forty years chasing his crazy Gomer in and out of impossible situations, loving her, loving her, loving her, with so little in return. It was hard to see, but it was there: the tenacity of God's love for a wandering, unfaithful people. For me.

Hosea's love for Gomer was very human. Her betrayals made

him crazy with grief and anger and prompted him to issue extravagant promises of revenge. He'd pout that she "went after her lovers, but me she forgot."[4] And in the next breath he'd "allure her...speak tenderly to her,"[5] then he'd run out and pay her bills, purchase her back from the pimp. All this is a literal description of what happened time after time with Mutt and Wendy. The utter *brokenness* of it—the conjoining of two lifetimes of dysfunction, codependence, and addiction—the abjectness, the lack of dignity with which Mutt/Hosea loved Wendy/Gomer... How could I see Jesus in this?

How not? All the words of Hosea—abject, angry, whiny, or tender—all are declarations of the Lord, according to the book that bears Hosea's name. Whose love is more transcendent, more truly human, more generously offered out of profound brokenness than that of Jesus?

Whoever has ears to hear, let him hear. Whoever has eyes to see, let her see the hidden Jesus.

Being: The Abandonment of Power

Being still enough, passive enough, to recognize the Jesus hidden in others helps me to move back into the activity of being the presence of Jesus in a much healthier, fuller way. When I see Jesus instead of just a poor, broken individual, it helps me resist one of the great temptations of ministry: the temptation to be powerful. How can I treat Jesus himself with condescension?

Power itself is not evil, of course. God is all-powerful, and Paul prays that we will experience in our lives the same power God used to resurrect Jesus.[1] However, most of the power we see exerted in the world around us, and that we seek to exercise in our own lives, is of a different sort. I am caught in a battle between the power of my own will and the power of the Spirit. They grapple within me like wrestlers: now one is on top, now the other.

My will seeks to dominate; the Spirit *emancipates*. My will tends to destroy or consume whatever gets in my way; Spirit power continually *creates*. My will defends itself; the Spirit calls me to enter willingly into the power of *vulnerability*.

God does not dominate us. On the contrary, he insists we make our own choices. Even when he does destroy something, he invariably creates out of it something new and even more beautiful than before. (He calls this redemption.) And, far from protecting himself, he hangs himself on a cross—and still allows us to reject him if we choose!

Choosing to be the presence of Jesus in this manner isn't easy. In fact, it's a kind of death. This way of being present requires me to increasingly deny myself and pick up my cross. It can be unpleasant lugging that thing around, and I drop it frequently.

Around midnight one late summer evening, I was finishing up some work in my "office" at Sanctuary. Sanctuary is a simple, old, evangelical-church building with a long, rather narrow auditorium, scabrous carpet, and tall multipaned windows of mottled glass—no stained glass—long since painted shut. A balcony overlooks the auditorium, and at the back of the balcony, or the front of the building, are more mottled-glass windows. These ones are made of small leaded panes, and the lead is slowly buckling under the weight of years. They do, however, keep out some of the wind. On this night, an exemplar of Toronto's reputation for humidity, I had one of the few functional windows in the building wide open.

The balcony, at the time, was my office. I shared it with Red Rain, the band that was the seed out of which God grew Sanctuary. More than half the space was crammed with amplifiers, speakers, a large soundboard, two shrouded lumps (keyboards and a drum kit under old bed sheets), and various other kinds of musical equipment. An Acadian flag was pinned to the ceiling at one end, and there were posters of Hank Williams Sr. and Billie Holiday at the other. Molding coffee cups abounded. My desk was in the corner nearest the stairs, piled with books, mail, and other papers. That's where I was sitting, plunking away at my laptop, listening with half an ear to the rhythmic swish of cars rolling past on wet pavement.

At first, the ranting voice outside barely registered. Many of our street people are deeply addicted, and others suffer from psychiatric illnesses. Ranting is pretty common. You get used to it.

Then I thought I heard my name. With my attention no longer locked on to the screen in front of me, I recognized the voice, too. Derek. My internal temperature jumped about ten degrees instantly.

❖

One afternoon during the previous fall, Derek had come to see me—sat right there on the ratty old couch and sobbed, peering at me through tears and a tangle of black hair.

"I'm afraid, Greg. It's getting so crazy out there!" Wringing his hands so hard the skin turned white as one twisted the other. Rocking back and forth, bending forward so far his beard brushed his knees. His voice rising in pitch and volume.

"I have to get out. You have to send me somewhere out of the city. I won't make it through the winter; I know I won't!"

It was a moment for which I had been waiting for years. I considered Derek a good friend, and I had already told one of my colleagues that I, too, was worried that Derek would not survive the winter. It wasn't just the killing cold; it was also the people he was hanging with. He was abusing himself and allowing others to abuse him to a fearful degree. Miraculously, I was able to get him into a program the next day.

He ended up at a rehab house in a town a couple of hours' drive from Toronto. I talked with him regularly on the phone, visited a couple of times, brought him home to our place for Christmas. He lasted almost four months before a government workers' strike put an end to one of the programs he was participating in. That became the vent hole for a whole mess of other frustrations— loneliness, an increasing trepidation about what would happen when he graduated, the fear of having to deal with the ugly stuff, long buried, which came bubbling up out of his past now that there was no heroin or crack or drink to keep it down.

Finally, Derek snapped. He found himself literally running from the house to the nearest drugstore. He bought a bottle of Listerine and drank it. Then he hopped a bus back to Toronto. By four in the afternoon, he was sitting in a doorway on Yonge Street with his upturned hat on the pavement in front of him.

As he sobered up a little, he realized he'd made a terrible mistake. He knew the rehab house wouldn't let him back in, even if he could make it back there. When Karen and Caleb found him squatting in front of the Thai restaurant, they invited him to come home to our house. By midnight, he was climbing into bed.

He stayed with us until early summer. There were a few slips here and there, but he seemed to be making progress—he'd got some work off and on, and had made plans to go back to school in the fall. Then he just bailed out, hit the streets again. And I was very angry about it.

Now here he was, standing below my office window at midnight, hollering insults and invective up at me. I leapt from my chair, ran to the window, and stuck my head out. Derek was walking away, still shouting obscenities over his shoulder. I shouted back.

"Hey—come back here! Don't you say that stuff to me and just walk away! You got something to say, come and say it to my face like a real man!"

He turned immediately and came stomping back.

"Something to say? Yeah, I got something to say! Come on down here and let me say it to you!"

He was rolling up his sleeves. I slammed the window shut and, mentally rolling up my own sleeves, ran down the stairs. I wanted to deck him. Just one good shot would be so satisfying! It's amazing how quickly the mind can process situations, though. By the time I was hammering the front door open, I was thinking, *I can't hit him. If I do, he will have won.*

Derek was better known for absorbing punishment on the street than dishing it out; in my anger, I wasn't afraid of his seriously hurting me anyway. But I knew that if I hit him, the whole street would know about it within hours. Many of them would even applaud me. But it would be disastrous—I'd have a steady stream of wired street guys stepping up to see if they could goad the preacher into a scrap. And besides, I had an inkling even then that what Derek really wanted was for me to punish him, lay a beating on him just as had always happened when he screwed up as a kid.

So I stepped out, spread my arms open wide, and growled at him: "You wanna hit me? Go right ahead. Take your best shot, man, 'cause you know—I won't be hitting you back!"

His eyes were bugging out like a couple of big brown marbles, his beard seemed to stick straight out from his chin, his fists were clenched and held chest high. His forearms were like braided ropes, blotched here and there by smudged blue-green jailhouse tattoos. His whole body was vibrating—I could almost hear it hum. He snarled and spit and gestured and used bad words. But he couldn't hit me.

He tried to walk away twice, but I kept calling him back, even calling him chicken once, telling him to come back and deal with it. And he did come back. He snarled and spit and cussed some more but still couldn't bring himself to hit me. At one point he gave me a little shove, but that was it. We finally wore ourselves out with the posturing. He stomped away, and I slammed the door on my way back into the building.

For a day or so, I felt like a hero, standing out there like that and offering myself up to take one in the chops. "Righteous" anger can feel so good. Slowly, though, the truth began its niggling little action on my heart and head.

I had known from the start that Derek probably wouldn't be able to hit me if I didn't take a swing at him. And I knew that, if he had punched me, it would be far, far more damaging to him than if I slugged him. He was much angrier with himself even than I was. Truly, he came looking for me to punish him—and I had. It would have been kinder to whack him a few times. In spite of all he had said, all the verbal abuse he had spewed, I knew he'd never be able to blame me for this silly little set-to. Whatever he said to me or anyone else, he would be telling himself how low he was for trying to hurt this person who had tried to help him, who had stood there and offered him a chance to take a poke. Derek was already in the gutter emotionally, and I had effectively stomped him through the grate and down the sewer pipe. At some level, I finally admitted to myself, I had known all this while it was happening.

A few months later, when we'd both had a chance to cool down and heal up a little, Derek and I got talking on the street. I asked him why he'd run away from our house in the first place.

"You had everything all set up," I said. "Place to live, work, school. You seemed to be really looking forward. So how come?"

"Greg," he said, staring at his feet. "I'm just a piece of s***, and this"—looking around at the garbage piled on the curb, the alleyway behind a strip club—"this is where I belong."

It wasn't true, but there really was nothing I could say. Everything I'd said and done to him during our altercation months earlier had been calculated to reinforce exactly that. How could I convince him now that he was precious, unique, made in God's image?

I had not looked for a way to emancipate him from the terrible feelings of guilt and inadequacy that bound him. Instead, I had thoroughly dominated him, making sure he understood with painful clarity that I was in the right. I had not sought to create a new hope in him, a hope that there might still be healing and dignity and forgiveness for him. No, I had crushed whatever scrap of hope might remain, cut another chunk out of a psyche already bleeding and barely alive. Offering to let him hit me was anything but vulnerability, even though it fooled both of us momentarily. I never let him see my own hurt, never confessed that I had seen his failure as my own. That I had deeply wronged him by viewing him as my project in the first place—which, to be honest, I had failed to identify in myself. I defended all of that by a calculated pretense of vulnerability that turned his anger back on himself yet again, driving the shank of his own self-loathing deeper, deeper. I had held my own power tight, refusing to release it even enough to ease his pain.

During his ranting, Derek had accused me of being self-righteous, a hypocrite, a fake—amongst other things! If I had been able to recognize his voice as the voice of Jesus, angry with the sellers in the temple using their position of privilege to rip off others, would I have run down the stairs ready to fight? If I had seen in his sense of alienation the forsakenness of Jesus, would I have been so quick to bait him? If I had recognized the presence of the Christ before me that night, would I not have had some possibility of being Jesus to him?

I am so glad that God is a redeemer, and that, even in this, I can trust him to bring something to life out of decay.

Seeing: The Power of Abandonment

The word *abandonment* generally carries negative connotations in our culture: spouses abandon each other; parents abandon children; people abandon cars, houses, and hope. But when I truly release my grasp on personal power—the power of my own will— I discover another side to the issue. I begin to discover that abandonment also means a wild, intoxicating release from inhibition —the abandonment of a passionate couple dancing to a Cuban band at a street party on a hot summer night. I begin to realize that abandonment can mean being freed from the traps inherent in seeking to dominate others, consume whatever is in front of me, or protect myself or my own agenda. When I step away from my fear that if I don't dominate others they will dominate me, and so on, I begin to discover true power, God's power—the power of abandoning myself into God's embrace.

Paul prayed that his Ephesian friends would experience God's "incomparably great power...which he exerted in Christ when he raised him from the dead."[1] They already knew the incredible power of his death: "redemption through his blood, the forgiveness of sins."[2] The resurrection power he wanted them to know in their

lives—right then!—sprang from Jesus's willingness to utterly abandon himself into God's—and humanity's—hands. His Upper
Room teaching is replete with this sensibility.[3] His garden prayer
with its simple, heartrending and exhilarating conclusion, "not my
will, but yours," is the statement of his intention to abandon himself. His arrest, trial, flogging, crucifixion, and resurrection are the
physical expression of it. And his final cry, "Father, into your hands
I commit my spirit!" is one of victory. The power of Jesus's abandonment would soon begin its regenerating sweep through all
creation.

The disciples couldn't see it at the time. The whole scene was
too shockingly tragic. It's not easy to see power in abandonment in
the painful mess of my world. But when I look for the presence of
Jesus in the poor and broken humanity within and around me, I
can recognize him in this indomitable drive to create, this joyous
compulsion to liberate, and a tender, courageous vulnerability.

CREATION

I'll never forget Patty's words when she stood to testify to our small
Sanctuary congregation just before being baptized. The words
sounded innocuous enough, and simple, but they cloaked a world
of painful complexity.

"When I was in a dark place, and nobody else could reach me,"
she said, "Jesus came and found me and set me free."

Few others present that day knew the story behind her seemingly stock evangelical statement. The "dark place" Patty referred

to was a rubber room in a psych hospital. Nobody else could reach her because she was often straitjacketed, and always doped to the gills. She had completely lost touch with reality—perhaps a blessing in the short run, since her reality had been so very destructive. Jesus first came in the form of a couple of members of AA, who pinned a towel around her neck to catch the drool when they took her out to weekly meetings. Patty was thirty-three years old.

She had been abused by her parents since she was an infant, and her bright, creative mind sought to protect that young self by splintering into a variety of personalities. The abuse at home continued throughout her growing-up years in a shocking variety of forms, and Patty was thoroughly convinced that she deserved all of it. Into her teen years, she sought men she hoped could save her. And, of course, they just abused her all the more. By the time she was twenty, she was a full-fledged alcoholic.

Ten years later, Patty was diagnosed as suffering from Multiple Personality Disorder. There's a different clinical name for MPD now, and much debate over whether it's a genuine psychiatric disorder or a condition brought on by questionable therapeutic approaches. But for Patty, it was simple. It was hell. She'd meet people for the first time, only to discover they felt like they knew her very well—and sometimes called her by a different name. She lost time—hours, even entire days, just disappeared from her recollection. She'd find herself in an unfamiliar place and not know how she got there, or realize she was bruised or broke with no memory of how it had happened. She regularly saw two psychiatrists and a physician, and each prescribed different medications. Patty was downing a cocktail of antipsychotic drugs every day, and her alcoholism was raging. Somewhere in there, a couple of marriages and two children went missing.

But think of it. Think of the incredible capacity for invention and improvisation required to create and sustain four or five distinct, fully realized characters, each with a history and emotional framework of her own. (There were more, but the others tended to be two dimensional, with very limited roles.)

This creativity wasn't limited to protecting Patty's own fractured person. As she began to get well, she began to look outward. Although she had often been at risk, she had never actually been homeless. Her connection to Sanctuary, and her growing appreciation of the gospel mandate to reach out to the poor, lit a little flame in her heart. She began to try to help others.

Sometimes she referred to Razzle Dazzle Patty, more a facet of her dominant personality than a separate one. Razzle Dazzle Patty loved to wheel and deal and make a big splash. She hunted gigs for Red Rain. She got next to some local radio personalities. She carried an attitude. She started an organization intended to bring together people and businesses wanting to help the homeless. One year, marrying several of her passions, she established the first-ever Toronto Beaches Blues Festival. Red Rain and several other bands played blues at Woodbine Beach to a few thousand listeners, and the proceeds went to help the homeless.

Because of her illness, none of the initiatives Patty started lasted very long. But she was loaded with ideas and a creative restlessness that meant she could rarely resist starting some new project. Her love for Jesus, and her desire to make sure other people heard about how he had set her free, was always at the heart of it.

The messiness, the incompleteness of her efforts, the parts that were driven by her own need to be "somebody"—it was easy to lose track of it in the midst of such confusion. But what could be more essentially Christlike than the urge, even in the midst of deep pain, to create?

LIBERATION

All this time, there was a war going on within Patty. Most of her alters (alternate personalities) were slowly quieted by her deepening commitment to Jesus, but one, Sara, was a "bad girl." It was Sara who generally got Patty into trouble with booze and men, and now she resented Patty's growing sense of moral responsibility.

Riverdale Park is separated into two halves by the Don Valley Parkway, one of the busiest commuter highways in Toronto. A pedestrian bridge connects the two halves of the park, crossing the northbound and southbound lanes of the highway, as well as the Don River, which flows beside them. It's a pretty spot, except for the traffic, with the park to the east and west, the valley stretching out to the north with the river winding along its bed. To the south and east, Riverdale Hospital and the infamous Don Jail perch on the border of the park; south and west, the office towers of the downtown core, dominated by the soaring spike of the CN Tower, rise above the brow of the valley, gilded by the setting sun.

It was just as the sun was setting, and the traffic had thinned out and sped up from rush hour, that Sara climbed over the low iron railing on the bridge and threw herself onto the northbound lanes below.

Sara apparently "died" in the fall; Patty did not.

Her legs were badly mangled. Her kneecaps were smashed and some other bones shattered. She endured several surgeries and bouts of infection that undid most of the benefit of the surgery. Within a couple of months, she had been moved to a rehabilitative hospital. Riverdale Hospital. Her room had a great big window, looking out on a beautiful park, a valley, and a river—and the bridge from which she had jumped. She tended to avoid the window.

Patty was not a model patient. In constant pain, barely able to move, unable to wheel and deal, and pretty much convinced she'd never walk again, she found the therapy sessions painful and fruitless. She found it hard to share a room with people who were brain-damaged and delusional. Many of the other patients had been there for decades, and their ailments were a catalogue of all the things you hope will never happen to you. Patty was crabby, often uncooperative, and always afraid. Afraid she'd never get out.

I was there once when Patty lit a cigarette for a friend and fellow-patient in the smoking room. Emaciated, thinning mouse brown hair, mouth open, and head propped against the headrest on his wheelchair. Just enough spark in the eyes to make it plain there was still a person in there somewhere. On a tray on the front of his chair, two hands like bundles of small dry twigs loosely held a curiously shaped glass dish with two spoutlike apertures. A clear plastic tube ran from one aperture into a hole in the flesh at the base of his throat. Patty got the cigarette going and, with a gentle joke and a pat on his arm, stuck it filter first into the second spout on the dish. It was fascinating and more than a little unsettling to watch the smoke fill the tube, then rush upward when he inhaled.

As time went on, Patty's condition stabilized somewhat but didn't improve much. She began to talk more and more about the people who had been trapped there for years. Some rarely had a visitor, others had family who would faithfully come on the week-end, bring flowers and sit beside a nonresponsive sibling, child, or spouse. The plight of people imprisoned in their own broken bodies and minds, then further trapped in an institution struggling with constant budget cuts and the threat of closure, began to weigh heavily on her. At least she had a realistic hope of being able to graduate from the hospital back into a place of her own someday. What about the others?

One day she left a message on my answering machine asking me to visit as soon as possible—she had somebody important she wanted me to meet. In the shade of the maple trees where the hospital property conjoins the park, Patty introduced me to Don. He was about the same age as she. He had a thicket of black hair, sparkling black eyes, and a motorized wheelchair. He had enough control of one hand to steer the chair, although not always very precisely—he clipped corners and rammed trolleys in hospital corridors fairly routinely. Most people could understand what he had to say only with difficulty, but Patty had learned to hear him accurately. Don had been a resident of the Riverdale Hospital for fifteen endless years, ever since getting mugged and being left for dead on a subway platform. Despite the devotion of two brothers, he'd long since abandoned hope of ever leaving.

Several months later, Patty and Don were married. In Jamaica.

Although she was confined to a wheelchair herself, with both unbendable legs sticking straight out in front of her, Razzle Dazzle Patty had found a way to spring them. It surprised everybody—they had been talking about marriage, but months in the future, maybe in the hospital chapel—and it was probably, in a number of ways, unwise. It was also incredibly beautiful. I've performed enough marriages to know that grooms in particular find the experience a little surreal. It's hard to believe it's actually about to happen, and that your life will never be the same again. I wasn't there, but I sometimes imagine how sweet and impossible and intoxicating it must have seemed to Don in that tropical garden in Jamaica, surrounded by swaying palm trees and the sound of ocean surf, filled with the knowledge that he was beloved of God, and beloved of Patty. Free. Free at last from long gray corridors and bustling uniformed officialdom and inflexible routine and cryptic announcements made over a crackling PA system. Free from the terrible weight of being forgotten, inconsequential. Free from the long, pale twilight of hopelessness.

When they returned from their honeymoon, Patty went to work again. Before long, she and Don moved out of the hospital and into a townhouse in an eastern suburb of Toronto. They invited a bunch of the Sanctuary crowd out for a celebration.

Surrounded by the friends Patty had introduced him to and

with their wheelchairs side by side, Don offered a simple toast: "We made it!" he crowed.

And *everybody* understood him.

Isn't that Jesus all over? Didn't he come right to where we are, experience our pain and hopelessness, then set us free? And isn't he going to appear some bright eternal morning and marry us and take us to our own home?

This is not a fairy tale. Nobody, in this life at least, lives happily ever after. After a couple of years, Don's health deteriorated, and he returned to the hospital. Patty actually walked into a Sunday service under her own steam one day not long ago, but since then the infection has returned. She needs more surgery. Their marriage often looks like a tiny boat negotiating a hurricane at sea, and their money is gone. But the reality of the miraculous liberation they have experienced still gleams like precious stones amid the wood, hay, and straw.

Vulnerability

If it's hard to see the creative and liberating power of Jesus inherent in truly abandoning myself into God's hands, it's more challenging still to embrace the concept of vulnerability as a kind of power. Still, it's very clear that Jesus was never more Lord and Christ during his life than at the moment of his supreme vulnerability. That Jesus himself was very much aware of this is abundantly evident in his every recorded utterance from the cross—think of his promise to the dying thief, or his intercession for those who "do not know what they are doing." Even the awesome power of the Resurrection is given its potency by the Cross that preceded it.

In Patty's life, vulnerability had always been exploited. Until she met Jesus, everyone she ever got close to had hurt her deeply. I don't suppose I'll ever really know how utterly terrifying it must have been to her to abandon herself into the hands of God, who had "failed" to protect her even as an innocent child. But I do know that I witnessed that abandonment, and with it a display of powerful faith that was a remarkable picture of Jesus.

Jesus's power to liberate me derives directly from his vulnerability on the cross. No death for him means no resurrection for me. Patty's story was no different. Long before she found a way to spring herself and Don from the hospital, she had endured her own passion…

The curtains were drawn against a bright afternoon sun, and the lights in the hospital room were off. The door was propped open, and a thin trickle of fluorescent light from the corridor seemed to sneak in behind me, as if uncertain as to whether it would be able to dispel the kind of darkness that had settled here. Patty lay curled up on her side, coverless, clad only in light underwear. Sweating. Her face was wet with tears, and she moaned softly.

I could hardly believe what I was seeing. One week earlier, Patty had been happy, steady, and eager to begin a new kind of therapy. A couple of years after she was baptized, Patty heard of a new clinic on the psychiatric wing of a major Toronto hospital that offered something called integration therapy for people who had been diagnosed with Multiple Personality Disorder. The basic idea was to take the alter personalities and, one by one, fuse them back together with the host or core personality. She had been anticipating a new level of healing and, because of the specific therapeutic process, a profound deepening of her relationship with God.

During her assessment, the therapy team expressed its surprise at her relative health and stability, given that she had never received any kind of therapeutic treatment for her condition. How had she managed it?

"I had help," she said, smiling. And she proceeded to explain to them the healing she had found in being held by a safe and loving community, one that encouraged her to continue to move more and more deeply into relationship with the Jesus she had come to love. This profound resting in the security of his love for her had begun to filter down to her alters and convince them that they were all precious and valuable and beloved. They became less fearful of Patty's being abused and so less likely to "take over." When she checked herself into the hospital to begin treatment, Patty was probably healthier than she had ever been in her life. The integration itself was to be accomplished through a symbolic act, something safe but powerful, a ritual that would allow the threatened alters (which were, after all, a protective fiction) a means by which they might blend right back into reality. Just what this act might be was still uncertain, and it was here that the therapy team graciously—and with great respect for Patty's spiritual convictions—invited my input.

As we encouraged Patty to identify the most powerful positive events of her pain-filled life, it became very clear that one stood out beyond all the others: Patty's baptism was the single most meaningful experience of her life. Together, we decided that baptism was precisely the symbol that could help her pass from the old death of fragmentation to a new life of wholeness. Two personalities would go down into the water together; one person would rise back up to a new kind of life. Patty was nervous, but excited about the prospect and delighted that this therapeutic work would be so directly connected to Jesus.

We never got to enact the symbol.

After she had been in the hospital just a few days, I was called away to a medical emergency in my own family. Now, a bare week later, just ten days after she had entered the hospital, I found a Patty who seemed shattered almost beyond recognition. It seemed incredible that, in an environment dedicated to her healing, she had descended into such darkness.

What had happened? I was told that while the psychiatrist was still conducting his preliminary assessments, Patty's psyche began to splinter again. The therapy team tried to calm her alters by finding and speaking with each one, to explain the process and its ultimate benefit. But the alters were terrified and rebelled. It was as if a brood of hyperactive children had hijacked the elevator and were running wild through the corridors of her mind. Patty's medication levels rose dramatically, and for a week she continued to spiral out of control.

Sobbing now, she told me how she had tried to escape the day before, only to be caught by a security guard at the top of a stairwell. He slammed her against the wall and threatened to throw her down the stairs if she tried to leave again. Then he dragged her back to her room. (Bear in mind, this was Patty's perception of the event, and she was terrified, exhausted, and more than a little disoriented. Still, it was frighteningly real to her.)

Earlier that day, she said, the head of the therapy team had come to her to apologize.

"Patty," he told her, "we seem to have done more harm than good. We've taken you apart and can't find a way to put you back together again. We're afraid that if we continue, we'll just do more damage. We think you need to go back to your community and just be with them. You've found more healing there than anywhere else."

Patty was wailing now. As she poured out her anguish, the room seemed to shrink and the darkness thickened. At first she was speaking to me, but before long she was crying out to God, pleading to know why she had been so forsaken. Where had he been when her own mother abused her as an infant? How could he allow the abuse to continue throughout her childhood? Where was the heavenly Father who was supposed to protect and cherish her? Why had every man she had ever turned to, right from her early teens through adulthood, looked like an angel at first, only to morph into a demon? Why had Jesus bothered to save her from the psych ward, only to dump her right back into the same hell now?

Why had the people who were supposed to help her turned into her tormentors? Hadn't she given her life to him? Hadn't she been born to a new life? Wasn't she supposed to be saved?

"So where are you now?" she cried. "Where are you? Where are you?"

God declined to answer.

I could do nothing but hold her hand and weep. There is no answer to that kind of complaint, or at least no answer one human being can supply to another. What happened next, however, was a miraculous and mystical reconciliation.

Slowly Patty's sobs subsided. The hospital sounds from the corridor—carts rolling by, muffled PA announcements, the occasional cry of another patient—seemed to die at the door to her room, emphasizing her isolation. Quietly now, and still sniffling, she spoke to God again.

"But I *know* you love me," she said. Sighing. "And I love you too."

It may have been the boldest, riskiest step of faith I have ever witnessed. Patty's complete and utter vulnerability, and the costliness of it, infused her acceptance of God's love and her confession of love for him with an unearthly power. The power of "not my will, but yours."

Patty did return to her community at Sanctuary, and she did, slowly, find a measure of healing there. It was after this that she began to display that indomitable creativity, and it was several years later that she found a way to liberate Don from his life sentence in the hospital. As I write this, it was just a few days ago that she unwittingly gave me the latest update on her embrace of vulnerability and the power that attends it.

I listened while, for the first time, Patty told someone she didn't know well about her jump off the bridge. The man she was speaking to was in distress, struggling with his own brand of hopelessness. "I still want to die every day, you know." She laughed. "I don't, though… My greatest victory right now is that I know how much Jesus loves me."

Coming from another mouth, those words could be just Sunday-school sentimentality. But they're so much more. They're words of power. The power of the Christ who abandoned himself into the arms of God, present and gloriously alive within Patty. Right before my very eyes.

Being: Picking Up My Cross

Jesus says, "Do you want to come after me? Be the next in line? You'll have to begin to lose sight of yourself and your own interests; you'll have to start to pick up your cross, embrace it, haul it around with you; you'll have to start taking the same road that I travel, walk it with me moment by moment. You'll have to lose your life for me, let it go, spend it, not try to keep it for yourself." Deny yourself. Pick up your cross. Follow Jesus. When he said this to his disciples, he had been talking about his impending death—a real downer; they were all embarrassed just hearing him blab about it like that—and Peter had responded by saying, "No way. Come on, Lord, this isn't going to happen to *you*." And so Jesus used that famous "Get behind me, Satan!" line, the strongest negative language he ever used toward his disciples, or anyone else for that matter. He made it clear that Peter's sunny view was straight from the pit. Then he described what it would take to really walk his path: death. Slow, painful death-on-a-stick.

And he upped the ante even more, going on to say, "When this is all over, I'm coming back. If you walk away from this, I'll walk away from you."[1]

As always, the cross is at the center of this way of being Jesus's presence in the world. It's the act of picking up my cross that makes it possible to connect the abandonment of my old self and interests with the possibility of truly emulating him.

"Deny yourself…" How completely antithetical to the society I live in! This means letting go of my "rugged individualism," my independence, my work ethic, my pride. It means not hanging on to old resentments, dependencies, excuses. It means concluding that none of these things define who I was meant to be, and it means beginning the serious, slow business of killing them off one by one.

"Pick up your *cross*." It's heavy; it's ugly; it's deadly. It's the stuff that pierces me, leaves me gasping in pain. The stuff that nails me in place and *will not let go!* It's the stuff that's gonna be the death of me. It's the shameful, humiliating stuff that I don't want anyone else to ever see, and at the same time it's the stuff that leaves me feeling utterly alone. "What if people knew what I'm really like?" And at the same time, "I wish there was someone else who knew what it's like…"

"And follow me." *Walk in my footsteps. Don't worry so much about the destination; be with me on the journey! Become the one I meant you to be in the first place, free of all the old restraints and preconceptions.* "Grow up…into Him who is the head, even Christ."[2] "Become" him, as a child becomes his or her parent. "Attain to the…measure of the stature…of Christ."[3] What a completely fabulous thought—that I might actually grow up to have the kind of maturity and beauty of Jesus himself!

But I can't attain to that stature if I simply deny who I am and have been! Can't just pretend all that ugly old stuff didn't happen or didn't affect me! And do I just walk away from my abilities because I'm proud of them—or disappointed in them? No... "Pick up your cross."

"Pick up *your* cross." My own cross. All the garbage and pain that is uniquely mine. The stuff that keeps me from being who I was supposed to be—and the stuff that, once redeemed, will turn out to be at the core of the identity God has had planned for me all along.

"*Pick up* your cross." There's no redeeming it if I don't pick it up, embrace that ugly, deadly thing, wrestle it onto my back. And stagger along with it.

◇

"Wanna see the scar?" he asks very matter-of-factly.

Three high-school students, two girls and a boy, are standing opposite him. They are stunned by what they've heard already, well into information overload, and now they can't believe what he's asking them. From somebody else the question might seem childish or boorish, but from Patrick, now, it's just one more exotic morsel he's put on the plate. For a moment they don't know how to respond—they're not sure if they should gobble it up or run to the washroom. Then they nod dumbly, mouths already hanging open a little. To refuse now would be to repudiate him after he's given so much. He's irresistible.

Patrick sticks the cigarette back in his mouth, pulls his shirt up and the waistband of his jeans down a little. They can see about five or six inches of the scar, relatively straight and thin, but clearly not surgical, a purple knotted line running through the fur of his belly. It starts somewhere up his shirt, gives his navel a little twist on its way by, and disappears down into his jeans.

The boy mutters something to himself and looks away. The girls just slowly lift their eyes back to Patrick's. They're not sure whether they want to touch him—or run away.

❖

Earlier in the day, Patrick had welcomed these three and about a dozen other students, plus one teacher, to the meeting room of Bridges for Youth. The students are from a Catholic high school in the suburbs of Toronto, and they are here to participate in what their curriculum calls a day of spiritual retreat. Bridges calls it Encounter Christ in the City. Patrick and other Bridges staff will lead the students through a briefing, a street walk, and a debriefing designed to increase their awareness of social-justice issues and challenge their personal faiths.

Patrick selects these three students and leads them out into a bright, clear November morning. He walks them through Allan Gardens, pausing by the trunks of some of the huge, bare trees that lurk in the dying park to light a cigarette and pepper them with information. He asks questions and insists the students try to answer before he gives the right answers himself.

"How many homeless youth—that's ages sixteen to twenty-four—do you think there are in Toronto? Don't know? Guess."

"Five hundred?"

"A thousand?"

"I dunno—maybe more than a thousand."

"How many students are there in your school?" Patrick asks them.

"Maybe about two thousand."

"Well, you can multiply the population of your school by about ten," he says. "There are about eighteen to twenty thousand homeless youth in the Toronto area."

The students raise their eyebrows. They find this a little hard to believe. She's polite about it, but one girl says she doesn't see that many homeless people around, let alone youth. Patrick listens carefully, nodding as she speaks. He pauses for a moment when she's done, then gently asks a question:

"Well, what about me? Am I homeless, or do I have a place?"

The possibility strikes them, and they really look at him for the first time. A small, trimly made man, shorter than any of them, close-cropped gray hair, wire-rimmed glasses. Thick, black eyebrows and dark, deep-set eyes. Hard to tell his age. Not old, but as they say, it ain't the years; it's the mileage. It filters through their thoughts that, although he's clean and neatly dressed, there's nothing he's wearing that couldn't be easily found at a thrift shop. Jeans, running shoes, a gray zippered sweatshirt. They can't tell, and they're embarrassed to guess. Patrick cocks an eyebrow, and with the nod of the head and the ghost of a smile, he leads them on.

The social-justice component of this particular walk focuses on homelessness and prostitution. Patrick is describing to them the different prostitution tracks visible from this park: the high track is over there; the price drops the farther away you get from it—by the time you get to that street over *there,* you're into low track, survival prostitution. Some girls there will go for a ten-dollar piece of crack. Up *that* street just north is the transvestite/transsexual stroll… See the green awning over the underground parking stairwell across the road? Okay, now turn around and look at the plaque screwed to the tree behind you.

Sean Keegan
1978—1996
Shot Dead

And Patrick tells the story of "Junior"—how Sean ended up prostituting to survive at age fourteen, how he called Patrick "Mom" and stole flowers and a Mother's Day card for him just days before his death because, he said, Patrick was the closest thing he had to family. How he curled up in a ball on Patrick's lap and sobbed when he found out—seventeen years old!—that he was HIV positive. How he'd discovered he could make more money if he went in drag. And anyway, the craziness of it kind of appealed to him. And how it all finally—but way too soon—came to an end at the bottom of *that* stairwell under *that* green awning with a bullet in the back of his head.

Patrick's quietness and gentleness are beginning to take on a different air to these students. They are beginning to recognize in him the authority of long and bitter experience. They are beginning to suspect there is more to come, that he offers far more than just a competent presentation of the facts. Repeatedly, when he offers them information that is shocking, or difficult to accept, he pauses and asks, "Are you guys okay?"

He shows them a few other spots not on the usual tourist maps. One is an alleyway that will become a workplace and a bedroom tonight. As they think about actually sleeping there, on the concrete, in the clothes they're wearing now, the pleasant coolness of the day seems suddenly chill. They actually shiver a bit.

Patrick scuffs at something on the ground with his toe. "Any of you have used condoms lying around on your bedroom floor?" he asks casually as he leads them away.

Waiting to cross Church Street, they bump into a young friend of Patrick's who cheerfully announces himself as homeless by describing how he just woke up in a nearby park. It occurs to one or two of the students that he is more expensively dressed than Patrick. After another couple of stops, the group pauses at a coffee shop for a break.

Patrick has a vat of coffee at his elbow and a fresh cigarette between his fingers. He blows out a mouthful of smoke, seeming to suspend the pale November sunlight as it streams through the windows.

"So," he says, still speaking smoke, "my name is Patrick."

The students know this already, of course, and they sense he is announcing something more—a shift, a new direction, a revelation.

"I was born and raised in London, Ontario. My father was a workaholic and an alcoholic; he'd work twelve hours, then come home and drink twelve beers. My mother was addicted to prescription pills. On my nineteenth birthday, I discovered that my father had two other families, and I had seven half brothers and five half sisters. I met some of them for the first time the next day. Others I'd known for years—I went to school with some of them—but I'd never known we were related. Neither had they.

"When I was four years old, an older brother began to physically and sexually abuse me. He offered me to some of his high-school friends, too. My parents were so out of it they never knew. Maybe they just didn't want to know.

"By the time I was six, I had discovered my mother's sleeping pills. I could take a few, go to sleep, and not feel anything for hours on end. That seemed so wonderful...

"When I was nine, I joined a men's and boys' choir. I enjoyed it, and I found a friend there—an adult who took an interest in me, drove me to practices and performances and so on. He was very good to me for two years. One evening, on the way home from a practice, he told me we'd need to stop by his mother's place. She was away on holiday, and he had to check on her apartment. I went up to the apartment with him, and there, for whatever reason, he raped me."

Smoke drifts aimlessly up from the cigarette resting motionless between Patrick's fingers. His voice is as quiet and gentle as when he was quoting statistics earlier. If anything, he seems fractionally more remote. The students are locked on to him, grappling with the dawning realization that this isn't just a story, and it's going to get worse. The girl who didn't think there were so many homeless youth finds herself wondering if anybody else in the coffee shop is hearing this—the guy sitting at the next table back-to-back with Patrick, for instance—and if so, what they make of it. He raises his head a little; sunlight flashes on his glasses, and he goes on.

"I never said a word to anybody. I don't know how my mother found out, but she did, and a few days later, she announced what had happened—to my brother, my father, my uncle, and all their coworkers while they were at our house for lunch. My father did nothing. My older brother, the one who had been abusing me, caught up with me later. He put a knife to my throat, drew a little blood, and told me, 'You weren't raped, you little bitch. You gave it away. You ever talk about that stuff again, me and my boys will show you what rape is all about.'

"I overdosed on sleeping pills that night. The good thing about it was that I discovered how safe it was being in a hospital— decent food, kind nurses, nobody abusing me. During the next year, I overdosed a few more times just to get back in there. Eventually, Children's Aid removed me from my parents' house and put me in a foster home. It wasn't much better there, so at twelve years old I hopped a bus to Toronto, the only big city I knew anything about.

"I was primed and ready for the sex trade. In fact, in a weird kind of way, it felt pretty good. Here, I was getting paid for what was taken from me by force at home. And there was some satisfaction in pleasing the client, getting paid for a job well done. Some sense that I was valued. For the most part, the johns treated me with far more respect and courtesy than my family had. And I had some street friends. Mostly, though, I was just beyond feeling anything much.

"I honestly didn't care whether I lived or died. When I was fifteen, I got picked up by what I thought would be an easy hundred-dollar date. He took me to a warehouse somewhere in the east end. He had a bunch of buddies waiting there, and for the next twelve hours they took turns raping me. I spent a couple of weeks in the hospital after that. Even went to the cops. They just told me, 'Look, kid, you know the risks. Get lost.' The long and the short of it, though, is that I was right back out on the stroll not long after leaving the hospital."

Patrick has led the silent group out of the coffee shop up and just off Yonge Street to a stretch of boulevard that is part of the "Boystown" stroll. The students hardly know where they are; they come to every few minutes, look around vacantly, and then lock on to Patrick again.

"By the time I was seventeen, I was doing the transvestite scene with a friend—my best friend at the time, and my roommate. One night we took a couple of dates back to our place. I got my date off without him even knowing I wasn't a girl—most johns know what they're buying, but these guys weren't too sharp. While we were doing our business, though, the other john had discovered the truth about my friend. He stabbed him to death. There was a big uproar, of course; it was all pretty loud and very messy. Somebody called the cops. They got there pretty quick, I must say. They caught and arrested the john, and I watched while they zipped my friend into a plastic bag.

"All I could think was, *How am I going to make the rent?*"

Patrick stops speaking, and slowly the students surface. The boy, a quick, lean Latino kid with a great smile and mop of curly black hair, swallows hard, shakes his head slightly, and turns to stare sightlessly at the stores across the street. The girl with questions about how many homeless youth there really are has more questions. She is polite and thoughtful, though, and she struggles with how to frame them respectfully. Finally, she just blurts it out:

"Didn't you feel *anything?* Couldn't you have done *something* to help him—gone to him, called somebody, something?"

"It was too late by the time I realized what was happening," he says patiently. "There really was nothing I could do."

Pause.

"And, no, I really don't think I felt anything much at the time."

But now, twenty years and more later, he finally turns away from the students, his mouth strangely twisted, his eyes suddenly red and full of tears behind the round glasses.

"So, are you guys okay?" he asks after a moment or two, not looking directly at them. They nod automatically.

There is a long silence. For a moment, the students are aware of the traffic lurching up and down Yonge Street just twenty or thirty feet away. Somebody asks one more question.

"How do you reconcile your faith in God with all the terrible things that have happened to you?" The girl with questions nods unconsciously. How indeed?

"Good question. Hmmm. *Really* good question... You know, when I was little, my grandmother used to take me to church pretty regularly. But I remember clearly when I had my first really conscious thought of God.

"Not long after I'd started working the stroll here—I was twelve years old—I got picked up by a date who, uh, wasn't happy with the way I did my job. He stabbed me in the stomach, then tipped me out of his car into the parking lot of a hospital. I remember lying there in the dark, trying to hold my guts in, and thinking, *So, this is it. God, what are you trying to do?*

"Wanna see the scar?"

After he's tucked his shirt back in and plucked the cigarette from his mouth, he continues, lifting his head a little to look each of them in the eyes. Not really a searching glance; more like he's checking yet again to see how they're doing.

"I was unconscious in the hospital for a few days, and when I came to, I had tubes coming out of every natural orifice in my body—and one or two that were new. But that thought was still there, and stayed. *God, what are you doing? Is there some kind of plan here, or what? If so, fine, let's get on with it. If not, please just let me go. I've had enough.* I really meant it."

Patrick sighs deeply, bogarts his cigarette butt into the street.

"Well, I didn't get any answers for a long time. I just survived, that's all. A few years ago now, my friend Rory—the director of Bridges—persuaded me to come and work with him. Bridges was located at Sanctuary at the time, so through Rory and the friends I met there, I started thinking about God again, for the first time in a long, long while.

"I guess I felt like I survived all that stuff for a reason. I'm still angry about a lot of it, and I don't know why it had to happen in the first place. But you know, it's *my* story, *my* life, and all those things have made me who I am now, so I'm thankful for that, thankful to be who and what I am. The whole thing"—he waves a hand, fingers splayed, in a wide arc—"has brought me to where I am now, right now, right here. So I can talk to you about things that really matter. All that nasty, painful stuff has meaning and value now. I can use it to help other people. God is redeeming it, and healing me at the same time."

Another pause. He looks carefully at each of them again.

"You guys okay?"

They nod mechanically. All of them look exhausted.

"Well, we have to go back now," Patrick says. "We still have to debrief with the rest of the class, and you haven't had any lunch yet."

He jams his hands into the pockets of his gray sweatshirt and saunters off down the street. The students follow a few paces behind, still not sure whether they want to touch him or run away.

One of the most incredible things about Patrick's story at this point in his life is that he tells it so often—generally three or four times each week. He does not do so without cost. A simple question from a student can turn the spotlight on a feeling, an action, or an incident that has lurked just out of sight in the shadows of memory for years and turn it into a sudden and searing pain.

Denying himself, for Patrick, certainly does not mean pretending he has forgotten the past, or that what happened doesn't matter. Nor does it mean that he gives up on his hopes for the future, or his present needs. He loves his work with the students—he is doing this not out of a sense of grim duty, but because he is convinced it is God's calling for him. Thousands of people with histories like Patrick's find within them reasons to abuse others, or themselves. Their lives may be dominated by anger and self-pity and self-destruction. Patrick, too, is very human. There are times he has to struggle to avoid lashing out at the students, simply because they are (relatively) innocent—they escaped, and he didn't. But Patrick is learning to abandon those old resentments and the attached self-definitions based on pride or shame.

Every time he retells a story from his past, Patrick picks up his own cross. By doing so he embraces his own suffering; he reminds himself, and declares to those who listen, "This is what I used to be. I am dying to this old stuff—a hard, long, painful death. I will carry many of these pains and all of the scars until I do physically die. In this suffering, I am entering into the fellowship of Jesus's sufferings, and he is making me into a new man, the resurrected man God means me to be. I am being transformed into the image of Jesus."

This is how Patrick follows Jesus, "becomes" him. This is the path he walks with Jesus, drawing closer and closer to his Father and home. For some people who have such a history, this level of disclosure would be humiliating and possibly dangerous; for Patrick it is part of "growing up into" God's image. As he walks around the city, he points out to the students the stations of his own cross; he offers up his own story of suffering to point them to Jesus. The students are often not immediately conscious of this, but I wonder: how many people who watched Jesus ben Joseph being driven through the streets and beyond the gates of Jerusalem to Skull Hill realized at that moment that they were looking at the Christ of God? Few of the students who have met Patrick and heard his story will soon forget him or it. Some, one day, will realize that they remember because Jesus was among them.

Seeing: Receiving the Gift of Life

The truly good news, of course, is that death is not the end. It is not the finish, and certainly not the goal. If Jesus calls me to carry my cross, it is so that I can live into these wonderful words of his: "I am the resurrection and the life. He who believes in me will live, even though he dies; and whoever lives and believes in me will never die. Do you believe this?"[1]

Yes, Lord, I believe. Help my unbelief!

When I go looking for Jesus, I go looking for the One who offers life. This offer of resurrected life is made directly out of his, and into the midst of my experience of pain and brokenness, fear and forsakenness. Nevertheless, it is also an offer that is made in joy, with joy as its goal—"that your joy may be complete!"[2] "Enter into the joy of your master!"[3]

When I am speaking to a church or other groups or individuals about Sanctuary and the pain-filled lives of some of our people, listeners will often remark, "I don't know how you do it. It must be difficult and depressing to be in the midst of that kind of suffering all the time."

I am no hero, and neither are most of the many other ordinary people who make up our community. Together, however, we are making some wonderful discoveries. By the Holy Spirit, Jesus is everywhere! He speaks through us and to us, constantly issuing this joyful invitation to truly live, to live a life resurrected and saturated with the eternal. One day we will enter this eternal life completely and finally—no going back! But even now, as we stagger under the weight of our crosses, he is pointing out to us the many places where new life is rising out of decay. The Sanctuary community includes many people whose personal histories are a litany of tragedies and abuses, but I have never been anywhere where I so consistently receive words of blessing and affirmation—the gift of life.

❖

Christmastime at Sanctuary is a riot of activity and emotion. And I do mean riot: it's big, unpredictable, loud, energetic, hilarious and tragic, exhilarating and often violent. Altogether, December is the most exhausting month of my year, both physically and emotionally.

As it is for most charities, it's by far our busiest month for donations. Food, clothing, money, sleeping bags, gifts, and offers of help stream in at a miraculous rate, challenging our resources to handle, store, and respond. It's truly wonderful. The experience of passing such bounty out to such needy people is a rare and touching honor. It's enough to cause you to sing "Glo-o-o-o-o-o-o-o-oria, in excelsis Deo!" And it's usually enough to help float us through the financial doldrums of the first quarter of the new year.

The other side of it, though, is that there is no other time of year when my friends who are stuck on the street, trapped by addiction and marooned by family, feel so completely useless. Rejected, on the outside of everything good and happy. Emotions are raw, and perilously close to the surface. Memories of Christmases past, whether fond or bitter, seem impossible to suppress and every bit as haunting as Dickens's ghosts.

Each year, it seems, some hard-bitten, long-term street guy snags me in a quiet corner of a drop-in and asks, "Can I make a long-distance call from your office?" The eyes and feet shift uncertainly, and I know that the call will be made to Mom or Dad, or son or daughter. It will be short, awkward, and very painful. This forty-year-old man who disappeared from Bohunkville fifteen years ago, and whose family hasn't known whether he is alive or dead for the last five years, will hang up the phone and stare at it for a minute before reporting, "The first thing she said was, 'Whaddaya calling for, money?' " Disbelieving, but knowing, of course that's what she'd say. Why would it be any different now? He'll wipe his eyes and nose on the sleeve of his jacket, or Burger King napkins if I have any, and ask if he can just sit on the couch here in my office for a few minutes. Can't go back into the drop-in like this.

The people of our community work hard to try to soften the harsher blows of the Christmas season for one another. We try to focus on Jesus, of course, and we pass around the largesse of our generous supporters. Those who have homes generally try to welcome a few more people in than usual. And like any other community, we throw a few parties. Traditionally, there's some kind of celebration on Christmas Eve, and another party specifically for the working girls (sex workers). There might be one or two other events as well, but the big one is always the Wednesday before Christmas.

We have a complete Christmas dinner: turkey with stuffing and gravy, cranberry sauce, potatoes and sweet potatoes, three or four other vegetable dishes, rolls, juice, coffee and tea, dozens of pies, platters of baking (donated or prepared at pre-Christmas baking parties), candies, and on and on.

This year each person received a beautiful and unique gift bag—a large, white paper bag with handles, decorated on both sides with a colorful drawing and Christmas greeting created by a child at a suburban church. The bags were filled with small gifts, useful and frivolous, and the handles were tied together with ribbon. One of our people, living in a hostel herself, pled for the opportunity to go out and buy Christmas cracker party favors, and so one lay beside each plate.

There was a huge evergreen wreath over the fireplace and evergreen garlands around the poles running down the middle of the room. Centerpieces with flickering candles on every table. And, of course, a fresh-cut Christmas tree. Two or three people were putting the lights on it, and the "Colonel" was trolling the room with a box of ornaments, insisting each person take one and hang it on the tree. The Colonel has long white hair and a voice like the last yard of gravel sliding off the dump truck. He's hard to refuse.

A small group flaked out on the couches and on the floor around the fireplace, dozing or chatting quietly. Popping sounds around the room announced the fact that some were snapping their crackers—they'd chuckle about the sad little pop! they made, laugh a bit when they pulled on the silly paper hats inside, groan when they read one another the jokes written on little slips of paper, and bicker about whose cracker had contained the "best" impossibly cheap and tiny plastic toy or puzzle.

Some of the people who were still sleeping outside received "Operation Good Thing" bags—street survival kits, including a sleeping bag, hat, mitts, socks, a flashlight, and a variety of other treasures supplied to us by our friends at Youth Unlimited. Some of our people had been out there long enough that the magic of these wonderful, once-a-year bags has worn off, but those who had never received one before slowly pulled each precious item from the black nylon duffel, considered it, and slowly packed it away again. Put the bag down by their chair. Touched it every couple of minutes. Moved it under the chair. Opened the bag up, took an item or two out again, put them away again.

Christmas music was playing gently in the background, the usual cribbage game was underway, grown men and women were poaching cookies and candies from one another like goofy children, light laughter and conversation rose from every corner of the crowded room. "Crowded" isn't usually good for us, and especially at Christmas when emotions are high, but this time was different. It was more than peace, which is precious and rare enough in our context. It was joy! The usual undercurrent of sorrow and anger was missing, and with it the clenched faces and forced smiles that are the standard markers of "just tryin' to get through this without taking a swing at somebody." There was an atmosphere of genuine and even slightly giddy celebration.

I may have been the only person there who was out of sorts.

The day before, I had received word that a friend of mine had died suddenly of a massive heart attack. We hadn't been especially close, but he had been the director of a drop-in program in a nearby suburban center. For about six months, he had been coming by to visit with me every few weeks to discuss some serious problems with that program, and I had come to appreciate his dedication and graciousness in the face of some major challenges. He was about forty years old, with no previous history of heart problems.

I could see all the wonderful stuff that was happening around me, but I couldn't stop thinking about his wife and two young children—a week before Christmas, choosing funeral options instead of trying to figure out how to sneak presents into the house. What kind of way was that for God to treat the family of a guy whose motto was "Here am I, send me"? A guy who gave himself heart and soul—literally!—to caring for people who are so battered they often can't care back, the people no one else wants to admit even exist? The people, incidentally, who God himself says he has a special affection for.

It was a little too close to home. I couldn't help but wonder what it would have been like for Karen and my four kids if it had been me. How would they ever manage to celebrate the birth of the Savior while mourning the death of their husband and father? My thoughts also slipped toward a meeting Karen and I already had set up for just a few days hence with another fortyish friend and her husband. Couldn't afford to let my thoughts rest there long, though. Doctors had told her she'd see one more Christmas, but they wouldn't venture an opinion much beyond that.

I've been angry about such things before, but at this point, I just felt weary and defeated. I found myself rehearsing the reasons why what we were doing mattered. I supposed it was still a good thing if my friends here at Sanctuary experienced some peace and joy, even if just for a little while, even if most of them still weren't able to connect that experience in any direct way with Jesus. I supposed so. It just seemed kind of pointless.

I had been upstairs helping some of my friends find what they needed in the mountain of donated used clothing. France, a friend from a small town north of the city, had arrived with some baking and other stuff for yet another party to be held Christmas Day and because she wanted to hang out for a little bit on this special day. We talked about family plans, the excitement of our children, and even about the peculiar emotional challenges of our kind of ministry at that time of year. As we walked back downstairs, I was accosted by Billy.

"Hey, do you wanna put some money on the Leafs' game?"

The only time in my life that I ever put money on a sporting event, I lost it to Billy. He's never let me forget it. When he told me he would be cooking for the drop-in on the Thursday night after New Year's, I responded that I expected to be sick that night and wouldn't be in to work—another running joke between us.

Billy was in his early thirties, a chunky, happy guy who appeared not to have a care in the world. He wasn't homeless, but I knew he'd been close a number of times. For years, he had led a life that revolved around bathhouses, bars, and late-night coffee shops. He had tried to connect with churches a couple of times before, only to be told that his sexual orientation meant there was no place in either the church or heaven for him.

He had started hanging around Sanctuary a few years before, slipping in and out of drop-ins. I'd bump into him on "the Steps" outside an all-night coffee shop on Church Street in the wee hours of the morning, and we'd spend ten or fifteen minutes yakking and bantering about nothing very important. He connected with other people in the Sanctuary community too and started to feel at home. One day he sidled up to me in drop-in. He was a simple, uncomplicated man, and he had a simple but serious question.

"Would I be allowed to come to the church here?"

We talked about his past experiences, and I realized that his question was much deeper than just asking about church attendance. What he really wondered was if there was a place for him in God's kingdom. Was it okay for him to ask questions and express opinions about God? Would it be possible for him to actually say that he believed in Jesus? Would Jesus be okay with that?

His humility was touching, but his sense of exclusion was heartbreaking.

Billy did find a spiritual home with us and discovered that Jesus was more than okay with Billy's believing in him. By the time of this Christmas party, he'd developed such a clear sense of his place and security in the community that he felt moved to explain a few things to France.

He threw a thick arm across my already heavy-laden shoulders and patted me gently on the chest with his other hand, booming at France.

"You see this guy? He's a friend of mine." He had no idea who France was. Kept patting my chest. Big grin. "He's a really good man. He's a great pastor."

The big grin was crumbling a bit, and he was suddenly blinking fast. He left off patting me to resettle the ball cap on the back of his head. Deep breath. People were going in and out of the door, up and down the stairs, all around us, but no one seemed to notice what was going on. Billy was oblivious to them.

"I was baptized here a year ago September! I love him."

Billy's face was confused. It couldn't decide whether to grin again or just go ahead and cry. He patted my chest once more and said, softly now: "He's a good man."

He introduced himself finally to France and shook her hand without really paying much attention to who she might be—"Nice to meetcha!"—then stepped outside for a smoke.

France left, and I finally made my way down to the drop-in. The tables were full, including a couple of extras that we had squeezed in. It was almost time for the meal to be served, and the noise level had risen to an anticipatory buzz. Every seat in sight was occupied, including the couches in front of the fireplace, and there were still a half-dozen people looking for a spot.

Many of my friends from the street have told me, "You can't starve in Toronto if you're willing and able to walk for half an hour." Churches, synagogues, social-service outlets, parachurch groups, and even the Ontario Law Society at Osgoode Hall (lawyers! Well, they should—our people provide a significant client base for those practicing criminal law) provide excellent meals for needy people. Since our perspective is that the meals we serve are most important for the opportunity they provide for the development of ongoing relationships, we normally insist that everybody— people from the street, kitchen helpers, middle-class community members or visitors, and staff members—sit down and eat together. As much as possible, we want our mealtimes to feel like they would in a healthy home situation. We sit in groups of about ten and serve one another from platters and bowls set on the tables. There is often some good-natured bickering about who will have to serve the others the main dish. Each group usually clears its own table, and individuals will fetch missing items or refill a water jug.

In a departure from our usual habit, the staff had agreed together that, for this particular meal, we would not sit to eat. Our expectation of a larger-than-usual crowd had been fulfilled, and although normally latecomers expect to wait until a place clears, on this day it had seemed important to squeeze in as many as possible at the start. I cruised around the room saying, "Hello, Merry Christmas!" and swapping jokes with my friends. Although I still felt outside it myself, the flicker of joy running through the room was palpable. Even more remarkable to me was the absence of tension, the usual sense that, while everything *looked* warm and Christmassy, something ugly might erupt any second.

Karen came from the kitchen and announced that the meal was ready to be served. Cheers from every quarter of the room. Normally, she will make a few brief announcements, welcome anyone new, and ask someone to give thanks for the meal. On this day, she took a huge gamble, telling a roomful of eighty or ninety hungry and excited street folks that she wanted to speak to them for a few minutes about what Christmas was really about and that, after that, Erinn Oxford (another staff member) would sing a song.

Throughout Karen's five-minute talk and Erinn's quiet song, I waited for the crowd to get restless and start whispering, snickering, or even talking out loud. Instead, there was a continued and attentive silence that could only be described as reverent—not a term we often use to describe our people.

As the food was being brought out of the kitchen (steaming platters and bowls, jugs of gravy, and the smell!) I resumed cruising the room. As I arrived at the corner table where I usually sit, I was surprised to notice one empty seat across from the Colonel and Brian.

Self-proclaimed leaders of "the Crest Crew," they were professional drinkers. Dedicated, unrepentant, and intelligent alcoholics. Whoever brews Crest strong beer ought to give them shares in the company. The Colonel was about fifty, Brian a well-worn thirty-something. I consider them both my good friends. We've buried a number of mutual friends and mourned them together through the years—usually deaths where booze or drugs played some kind of role—and, as painful as that is, it does forge a bond.

"Hey, guys!" I said. "How did that chair manage to stay empty? Lemme get someone to fill it."

As I turned to wave a waiting guest over, I heard a chorus of "No! No!" behind me. I turned again to face them.

"That seat is for you!" the Colonel said, rising partway out of his seat and indicating the empty chair with an elegant dip of his trembling hand.

Brian cursed merrily and waved his arm to indicate the crowd in the room. "Do you know how many people wanted to sit there, and we had to tell 'em to, uh, hmm…go elsewhere?"

I was about to say thank you and decline, but the words died on my lips. It dawned on me that they had been defending that seat against a horde of hungry street people for about an hour and a half. I had no choice but to bow to their determination and affection. I sat down.

The meal was glorious and silly (the Colonel wore a yellow crepe-paper crown over his Montreal Canadiens cap) and incredibly filling, of course, and just beautiful in every way. Each person at the table seemed intent on serving the others with a polite gravity and attention to every need that would have done credit to an old-world butler. It was a little surreal, frankly: hardcore street guys used to scrapping for every square foot of pavement, treating one another like rajahs. But it was wonderful.

Brian and the Colonel doted on me. They filled my plate, told me stories, and laughed at my jokes. They offered me every delicacy on the table before I was aware of wanting it. About ten minutes into the meal, as he usually does, the Colonel wavered to his feet.

"Okay, people!" he shouted into the room. "It's time to say thank you to the beautiful people who made this beautiful meal for us! Look at it! The turkey and stuffing…"

He went on to describe in detail what was directly in front of each person there. There was laughter and catcalls and shouts, and very specific suggestions as to what the Colonel should do with his own dinner, but when he was done, the room erupted in applause and people thumping tables.

Memories like that are gems. You might toss them in a drawer and forget about them for a while, and when you pull them out, you might have lost some of the details about the setting, but the gem itself never loses its shine.

When people had begun to groan and push their plates away—but before the forty-odd pies and ice cream and the plates of baking came out—Santa burst into the room. Even from a distance, it was obvious that his suit was cheap and flimsy, his patchy beard was askew, and his large stomach was suspiciously square and pillowlike, but he more than made up for any lack with energy. If I had seen someone leaping about like that on the street at night, I would have assumed he'd just smoked a twenty-piece of crack, but I knew it was just Billy's excitement. His appearance was greeted with a roar of delight, then more laughter and exclamations as he began to hand out the white gift bags.

The afternoon rolled on and wound down. Only a handful of

people were left chatting quietly at the tables or flaked out on the couches when Donald sat me down for a chat.

He was a big man. Large enough in any direction you'd care to measure him to have acquired the inevitable big man's street tag: "Tiny." He had begun coming to Sanctuary a few years before, looking as if he wished he could slide in unnoticed. At first he didn't come often, and then only for lunch on Wednesdays. I clearly remember his first visit, though. Generally, it takes our crowd a long time to trust anyone enough to share important personal information, but within minutes of meeting me, Donald told me that his wife had died not long before. He'd lost his job and was living at Seaton House, the largest men's hostel in the city. He had been wrecked by his experiences, and was obviously a man adrift. He seemed apologetic just about being present.

Through the years that followed, Donald slowly found his way deeper in toward the heart of the community, and his sense of God's presence and activity in his life grew. He moved to a clean, safe rooming house and made some friends there. He began to realize that he had gifts to offer as well as receive. When the Sanctuary kitchen was renovated and expanded in the early part of 2001, he found his own special place there and a special friendship with Karen. At a celebration for the official reopening of the building that June, he stood proudly at the stainless-steel island with his friend Jonathan and served the cookies they had baked to Ontario's lieutenant governor, Hilary Weston.

Donald had helped plan and direct several baking parties to prepare pies and baked goods for the Christmas party. He had helped plan the menu for the dinner itself, and he'd been part of the team that did the actual cooking and serving. He had also approached Karen to talk about the possibility of cooking and serving dinner on Christmas Day for the men at the rooming house where he lived. *Sixty* men. (He did just that, by the way—mobilizing a group of other residents and transforming a house where silence, solitude, and firmly closed doors had been the immutable Christmas tradition for years.)

Donald was a man transfigured, a life resurrected. When he sat me down that day, he wasn't seeking pastoral care from me. His purpose was to pour out blessing on me. He told me in great detail what our relationship had meant to him. He spoke of small kindnesses I had long forgotten, expressions of spiritual challenge and encouragement I had offered, the sense of welcome—the sense of home!—he'd had from the first time he stepped through the doors, the many small opportunities offered to engage in the life of the body of Christ. He reminded me of introductions I had made that had led to other important and healing relationships. Ours wasn't the only relationship that had helped him recover his life, but he had chosen this moment to bless me specifically with his gratitude and affirmation. As he spoke, I realized that I had done nothing extraordinary and little that required any special effort, wisdom, or giftedness. God had met and blessed Donald in the midst of our friendship. Now Donald was blessing me back.

Donald, like many of us, found it difficult to accept praise for his own abilities or person, and I had spoken to him a couple of times about how important it is to allow people to bless you like that, and to try to receive graciously what they offer. So he smiled as I squirmed under the onslaught of his blessing for me.

Billy, the Colonel and Brian, and Donald had no idea what I was struggling with that day. In fact, it's entirely likely that they didn't know I was struggling at all. They probably had no sense that they were doing anything extraordinary. Each in his own way was just saying a simple thank you. But to me, at a time when my spirit was wounded and preoccupied with death, they spoke words of resurrection. They offered me new hope, new life. And each of them offered these precious gifts out of his own pain and suffering.

In Billy's simple, heartfelt statement, "I love him," I can hear the voice of Jesus saying, "As the Father has loved me, so have I loved you. Now remain in my love"![4] This is an invitation to live a new kind of life, a life in which I am continually surrounded by Jesus's love.

In the Colonel's and Brian's insistence that I join them at the table, I can recognize the eternal invitation, "Come; for all things are now ready!"[5] Jesus wants me to sit at the table with him, now and forever, feeding on his presence instead of starving my soul while I run around managing everything.

Donald's blessing is a reminder that Jesus's life is growing in me, even when I am unaware of it. And it's that growth that produces fruit—the evidence of life! I am (slowly, slowly) growing up into his image.

I never got any answers about the death of my one friend, or the terrible trial awaiting the other. I do know that in the midst of my own struggle and discouragement, Jesus made himself present to me. I can trust that he made himself just as present to the ones I love, and will continue to do so. And as he made himself present to me, he offered me, yet again, the gift of resurrected life. I won't experience that life fully, of course, until the final resurrection, but the tasting of that heavenly gift in the here and now nurtures within me a hunger for the incredible feast that awaits.*

---

* Ironically, Brian died just before our 2002 Christmas party. He and the Colonel had panhandled enough money for a cheap hotel room and a box of beer. They drank themselves to sleep, and Brian never woke up. A teary memorial at Sanctuary was followed by a ritual drinking bout in the park next door. I miss him still.

And Billy, our first and only Santa for Sanctuary Christmas parties, missed the 2003 party. He was in intensive care, fighting for his life. A Santa suit Karen had made for him was draped over a chair at the front of the room while 175 of us shared Christmas dinner. Bill passed away a couple of weeks later, succumbing to pneumonia and cancer brought on by AIDS. He was afraid, but confident that he was secure in the arms of his loving Father. His funeral was held at Sanctuary—a joyous celebration of a simple man by a stunningly diverse group of people. I look forward to seeing him again some day.

Epilogue: The Surprise of Brokenness

In the church where I was raised, we were taught always to refer to God's Son as the Lord Jesus Christ, or at the very least the Lord. The stress was always laid on his uniqueness, his perfection, his deity. To refer to him merely as Jesus was considered to be disrespectful at best, and charitably as a sign of either spiritual immaturity or shallowness.

I believe with all my heart that God's Son is Lord—Lord of lords, King of kings, the Word, the One by and for whom all things have been created and are sustained. He is the Lion of the tribe of Judah, and the fearsome figure whose tongue is a double-edged sword, whose voice is like the rushing of many waters. He is the White Horse Rider, faithful and true, who judges and makes war with justice. He is the light that illuminates the New Jerusalem and every individual who comes into the world. He sits on the throne of heaven and on the Great White Throne of Judgment.

And I believe, often with the desperate gratitude of one dying of thirst who has just been given water, that he is the Christ—the Anointed One, God made flesh, God among us, Savior, Redeemer, High Priest and sacrifice, Author of Salvation, the Lamb of God who takes away the sin of the world—my sin! He is the Righteous One, who speaks in our defense, and offers his own blood for our cleansing. He is the Holy One of God, the Living Water and the Bread of Life.

Each of these roles of the Lord Jesus Christ is unutterably precious. But I am so glad that, when he calls me to follow him—to be his presence—he is not asking me to try to assume any of these roles myself. I am not judge or savior; in fact, I am never so clearly wandering from The Way as when I try to be one or the other. One of the most important things for me to remember about being Jesus is that I'm not Jesus!

It is, however, *Jesus* that I'm invited to emulate. Whoever wrote the letter to the Hebrews made it clear that we don't yet see him in his exalted roles as Lord and Christ—"At present we do not see everything subject to him. But we see Jesus, who was made a little lower than the angels,"[1] representing and tasting death for every human being. By saying that we don't see him exalted yet, I think, the writer means simply that those aspects of his person are just too big for our wildest imaginations to encompass. Jesus the man, though—him we can imagine. It's Jesus, the carpenter (no capital letter) of Galilee, who was materially present in this world, walked the dusty roads, got thirsty and hungry, felt angry, alone, frustrated, and betrayed. This is the man who died a lonely, humiliating, and gruesome death, and it is this Jesus whom God made perfect through suffering. This Jesus is not ashamed to call me his brother![2] (And the author of Hebrews was not ashamed to call him Jesus with no other qualification.) The writer goes on:

During the days of Jesus' life on earth, he offered up prayers and petitions with loud cries and tears to the one who could save him from death, and he was heard because of his reverent submission. Although he was a son, he learned obedience from what he suffered.[3]

If you had asked me when I was, say, twenty-five, how I could be the presence of Jesus, most of what I would have told you—assuming I understood your question at all—would have centered on ways I could possibly have modeled his strength, purity, or faithfulness. And if you had gone on and said, "Where or how do you think you could see him in other people?"—well, I would have thought you were talking gibberish, to be honest. But if I had been able to get my head around the question, I would likely have said something about seeing that strength, purity, and faithfulness at work in others.

Of course, the biblical writers encourage me to be strong (in the Lord, and in the strength of his might, according to Paul[4]), exhort me to be pure, and call me to faithfulness. These are the behavioral goals to which I ought rightly to aspire.

However, these stories of my friends reveal a peculiar paradox: I am more likely to have Jesus revealed to me and through me in weakness than in strength, sinfulness than in purity, or doubt than in perfect faithfulness. If I can sum up all these "failures of the spirit," all these ways in which nothing ever seems to work the way it should—not the people around me, not the sequences of events that I witness or in which I find myself engaged, and certainly not the operation of my own contrary heart—if I can sum up all these things with the single term *brokenness,* then I come to this astonishing conclusion: Jesus is found in brokenness.

This is the surprise of brokenness. The all-powerful Lord may seem distant and even frightening; the spotlessly perfect and unique Christ may seem unattainable. But I know what it's like to cry out in desperate prayer; I, too, seem to need to suffer in order to learn how to be the Father's obedient child—although, unlike the Son, it's generally my own sins that cause my suffering. It's the broken Jesus whom I can approach and even, in some small way, begin to emulate. It is he who connects me to the Lord and Christ.

The surprise of brokenness is not just that the Almighty allowed himself to be broken, and that he invites me to touch him there in that brokenness. It's also that my own brokenness—that hidden, ugly, twisted stuff that I had expected would disqualify me forever from his friendship, and that, if it were known, would torpedo all my other relationships too—is precisely the place where he desires to touch me, and it is the place where I am most able to truly connect with other people.

My brokenness, then, turns out to be *a place of meeting.* My friends from the street keep me at a distance as long as they consider me to be whole and holy; when they discover the truth that I am messed up too, we find common ground.

Shortly after writing it, I gave a draft copy of the story of my almost fight with Derek to a friend to read. He had come from the street, was valiantly battling addictions, and had been speaking to me about the riot of resentments he was experiencing in dealing with some of his past associates. I had told him several times that I often experience similar feelings myself, but that seemed difficult for him to accept. Many of my street friends seem to think that because I am a pastor, I must be of a different species from them and perhaps not capable of the same kind of emotions, instability, or dysfunction. By nature, I'm not inclined to quick displays of anger, and I've had years of experience dealing with truly objectionable people and situations in a (mostly) calm manner. Although he knew me well, the story was a surprise to my friend. And it was a gift. To both of us. He understood immediately that I was choosing to make myself vulnerable to him, and he treated that confidence—and me—with supreme tenderness. It encouraged him to know that I really do share some of his struggles and helped him to see that they are part of the human condition, not just more evidence that he himself is a screwup.

As long as I pretend to myself and others that I am "just fine, thanks," I keep people—and even God; especially God!—at a distance. When I admit my brokenness and enter into more intimate relationships with God and his people, I am less inclined to judge others' brokenness. Instead, I can *dignify* it, recognizing and mourning the deep pain and alienation that is the inevitable result of being sinful people living in a sinful world but rejoicing also that we are together in this, and that God is with us, meeting us at the very point of our need. Essentially, this is simply the practice of confession, and confession is truly good for the soul. It releases me from the pressure of having to pretend that I am other than I am. And that honesty forbids me from requiring very much of others.

When I see that my brokenness, once acknowledged, becomes a place of meeting and an opportunity to dignify rather than dismiss or degrade others, I discover also that my heart soars with the great hope that all my brokenness is ultimately *redeemable* in other ways as well. What God doesn't finally burn away, he will turn into gold and silver and precious stones.[5] He will perfect me, too, through this suffering. My suffering, my brokenness, will ultimately be much more than merely a series of painful experiences and personal failings to be survived; by the alchemy of grace, God will transmute it all into something of eternal value and beauty.

Suffering without meaning is the path to despair. Suffering with meaning is the trail to glory. And Jesus is the pioneer on that trail. There's no place we can go that he hasn't been already.

A PLACE OF MEETING

Strange how often he shows up on the streets on those ugly nights when sensible people just stay home. It's mid-November, close to midnight, and the cold has yet to reach a clean, true-winter snap. For now, it's just that subversive, raw chill that seeps upward from the sidewalk and spreads through your feet, legs, up to your shoulders, and down to your hands. It's not until your fingers are aching with it that you realize it's not just cold *out,* you're cold right through too. If there's going to be precipitation—and it feels as if there could be at any second, though the pavement is dry—there is no way of knowing whether it will be rain or snow or a sheet of ice creeping down Church Street from the north.

Rose is a high-track girl for sure, and she stands her corner with all her might. She has a tumble of Hollywood blond-streaked hair, perfectly painted lips, and long legs that rise from thigh-high, shiny white, stiletto-heeled boots to disappear into an astonishingly brief pair of shorts. A waist-length fur jacket, generously open. And some kind of bustier, which you can't afford to inspect too closely, that offers the rest of her (including a small namesake tattoo) to the world.

When you get up close, Rose's eyes are the best part of her. Luminous hazel irises precisely painted onto whites as clear and glistening as porcelain. If eyes are the windows, there's no doubt this one has soul in abundance.

No body is perfect, and she's not a kid any longer. When Rose turns to talk to someone else, you can see that the shape of her nose displays evidence of having been surgically altered—a rough kind of surgery, the kind administered in a hotel room by an angry pimp or john. Her teeth are a peculiar streaky gray, her inheritance from a heroin-addicted mother. It's a testament to her character that despite everything, she never hides those teeth; she laughs and smiles as freely as a little girl. You love that about her.

She greets you and your street-work partner with an enthusiastic but strangely motherly hug, asks after your spouse and your "beautiful little babies"—it doesn't matter what the ages of your children are; she always refers to them that way. You tell her how the kids are doing, the little things they're into, how they've grown and so on, because you can see that she's not just being polite, she really does want to know. It strikes you that this is the kind of conversation you'd expect to have in the foyer of a church, after the service, with one of those beautiful old saints with tight white curls, arthritic fingers, and a row of imitation pearls.

Rose is a mother too, so you ask about her kids. Those great hazel eyes brighten another dozen or so watts. Oh, Jas is into the terrible twos now, he's *so* much trouble, she tells you, chuckling. And Reuben! Nine going on eighteen, handsome as his father, but without the temper so far, thank God. The school says he has an attention deficit problem, but they're working with him, and he seems to be doing a little better. On she goes with the details that occupy any parent's attention, and you can tell that, despite the fact that nobody anywhere ever has modeled healthy parenting for her, she is absolutely dialed in to those children.

You make some remark to that effect, and her eyes fill with tears. "I love them," she says, simply, softly. "I'd do anything for them."

And she does. Every night, in cars, hotel rooms, alleyways. Every night, she sacrifices her body for the children she loves.

She tells you that Reuben saved her life. The father could see a six-month interruption of his principal income on the horizon when she told him she was pregnant. He alternately offered her the world and threatened her life so she'd go for an abortion, and she actually got on the bus one day to go to the clinic. Then, the strangest thing happened.

Somebody spoke to her—not somebody on the bus, or waiting for it, not somebody she could even see, but somebody definitely spoke to her. This voice told her that she had to give birth to this child and keep him. He would save her life. And that's exactly what happened.

When the father realized Rose was determined to carry the child, he simply walked away. Everything about their history together suggested that her expectations of beatings and worse would be fulfilled, but instead he walked away. And when Reuben was born, it was as if she herself had been granted a new kind of life. She had a reason to live.

She's sure, she tells you, stepping a little closer and looking you straight in the eyes (trembling lips, flicking a tear away with a long plastic fingernail), that if she had aborted him, she'd be dead now. He, and now Jas, are still her reasons to live. That Reuben! He's such a little hunk. A tiny, one-note hiccup of a laugh.

She sighs, looks down, suddenly deflated and weary.

"Can't believe I'll be thirty in a couple of weeks," she says. "Thirty! I can't believe I'm heading into my eighteenth winter out here..."

She inspects the street and buildings around her critically, as if it's the first time in a long while she's really looked at them. It all seems suddenly grayer, as if you were watching television and someone had fiddled with the contrast controls. The question flutters through your mind: Which is more heartbreaking, the last eighteen years, or the first twelve?

Rose says she'd get out if she could. But who would hire a thirty-year-old woman with no schooling and no résumé—not one you could attach to a job application, anyway! She tried once. Actually got a job as a cashier for a couple of months. But after years of working the street, she felt like she was on a different planet. Couldn't maintain any kind of focus and couldn't make enough money to pay the bills. Still, if it weren't for her boys, she'd pack it in. (You wonder if "packing it in" refers to sex work, or life in general.) It's the only way she knows she can make enough to support them. She shakes off that line of thinking with a kind of controlled shiver. She glances around again, and it seems to you that this time she's wanting to be sure that no one else is close enough to hear what she's about to say.

"I gotta tell you something," she says, almost whispering. "But you'll probably think I'm crazy." Glancing over her shoulder again and leaning still closer.

"I think…" The pause tells you she's concluded she can't actually say it, but then she gathers herself together again.

"I think God talks to me sometimes."

She's looking at you, those fabulous eyes glistening again, waiting for you to find some gentle way of telling her she's nuts. You're faintly surprised to discover that this makes perfect sense to you, that God talks to Rose, and you tell her that. Of course he talks to her. He loves her. She's inspecting you to make sure you're not just condescending to her little fantasy. Apparently satisfied with what she sees, she continues. It seems she missed the "love" part.

"I think he likes me, too." She's not saying this with that defensive you-know-I'm-actually-a-pretty-good-person kind of attitude. This, apparently, is mostly what God has to say when he talks to her. She seems surprised and touched, as you would be if someone you thought had never known you were alive expressed his or her undying affection for you.

Suddenly, you realize that she has assumed that God talks to *you,* and likes *you*—of course he does; you're church people. She's always believed that God speaks to his people (church people; not the phony ones, but the ones who are sincere and have their lives all neat and tidy) and loves them. It's not bordering on *crazy* to think that God would talk to somebody like you—the surprise is in discovering that he includes *her!*

Rose's humility shines a penlight into that dim corner of your soul where you have so carefully stashed your arrogant assumption of God's favor. Although the assumption itself holds true, your arrogance crumbles. You find yourself stumbling over words, trying to express to Rose just how precious she is, how clearly her passion for her children speaks to you of the passion Christ endures to bring his sons and daughters to glory. You want her to understand that God doesn't just like her, he *loves* her, spent his Son for her, that there *is* forgiveness, that the new life she sensed at Reuben's birth is just a taste, merely a whiff, of the feast he wants to spread before her.

This is a little much for Rose. She doesn't get it, and she treats you to the kind of nodding smile reserved for silly but well-intentioned flattery. She gives you and your partner maternal little back-patting hugs that imply a gentle but distinct dismissal. She's looking past your shoulder at the cars cruising by. She sighs something about renting body parts and, with a final wave, steps toward the curb.

DIGNITY

Alphonse and Little Johnny operate in seamless unity behind that long counter, two bodies controlled by one mind, offering up their nightly ministrations of cheeseburger voodoo. Johnny drops the basket of fries into the hissing grease while Alphonse is taking another order, but it's Alphonse who retrieves the fries a couple of minutes later. He lifts the basket from the fryer, dumps the fries into the bin, and waves the saltshaker over them without even glancing down—his attention is fixed on the hockey game being shown on the television hung high in the far corner. Vancouver is spanking a Detroit team that has not yet begun to take the play-offs seriously. "Fishburger and rings!" shouts Little Johnny. By the time the customer arrives at the counter, it's Alphonse who is standing, indicating the condiment choices with a wordless flick of his wooden spoon.

Below the hockey game, four or five women sit before video games, smoking and chatting casually as their fingernails click on the glass screens. They have played these games hundreds of times, and the bright images occupy no more of their attention than breathing. A few more women sit at nearby tables picking at plates of fries and sipping beer or hot chocolate. Nobody buys Johnny's coffee. A young woman in sweats and a chemical tan slides by the table, flashing a grin at you and your partner as you sit talking with another of the working girls. A few minutes later, you decide it's time to get back out on the street, so you excuse yourselves and get up to leave.

On your way out, a new woman sitting a little to one side of the others by the games speaks up:

"You work with Steve, right? You're the church people?"

Steve is Sanctuary's street pastor. At about six four and two forty, with a bushy, graying beard, he stands out. He looks like a member of Hell's Angels, but the women here know him as pastor and friend. Even women new to the stroll get to know who he is pretty quickly, and the woman speaking to you is definitely somebody new.

She seems a little self-conscious, so you step closer. She turns a bit so her back is to the rest of the women. Introductions all around—very formal, complete with little handshakes—and Carmelita tells you she's asking because she's kind of interested in going to church, but she needs, you know, to find a place where she wouldn't feel, like, singled out.

You tell her about the worship time at Sanctuary—"Oh, at 5:00 p.m.? That'd work, 'cause I'm not really, you know, a morning person"—and assure her that her situation would not be unique in the congregation.

As you take your leave, the young woman with the grin swings out of the restroom hallway. The sweats are gone. Now she's dressed mostly in the chemical tan, augmented by a little spandex, high heels, and a couple of pounds of artfully applied makeup. Although she's wearing much less, her self has been cloaked. She grins at you once more, the momentary flash of a carefully hidden soul. Your partner holds the door open for her, and you follow her out to the street.

◆

Over the next couple of weeks, you see Carmelita on the street, but she's working, and there's little opportunity to talk. It's not until you meet again at Little Johnny's that you really connect.

She's a pretty Filipina, early thirties, with clear coffee-colored skin and a big smile full of perfect, sparkling white teeth. Black hair pulled straight back from her forehead, bursting into a mass of curls at the back. She's dressed quite sensibly, except for the standard extravagant cleavage.

You talk first about church stuff again, and she explains that she lives out in suburbia and doesn't have a car. Sanctuary sounds like it would be a good fit for her, but it really doesn't work for her to actually get there on any kind of regular basis. Would you know of any place closer to where she lives that she'd be welcome? You tell her you'll make some calls, see what you can find. You ask about her living situation, and she tells you she's been staying with her parents.

"Do they know what you're doing here?"

"Oh no!" Mildly shocked. "They'd just die."

All through this conversation, Carmelita's been engaging, intelligent, and breezy, but you have the sense that she's jockeying for position, trying to find a way to talk about something else a little closer to the bone. Her eyes flick back and forth around the restaurant to see if anyone is paying attention. The other women are engaged in their own conversations, and the ubiquitous night creatures—sweaty men who sit drinking beer a few tables away from the clutch of women, greedy eyes roving from body to body—well, they're paying attention all right but not to anything she might have to say.

After a few more polite but meaningless exchanges, and with absolutely no change of expression, she sallies forth.

"I don't really feel like I fit, you know?"

"How so?" you say, thinking she's returning to the church discussion.

"Well, look at these girls. They all seem to have it so together—you know, they always seem so happy and carefree, and they keep themselves looking so good. I just always feel like I'm falling apart." She says this all casually, bright-eyed and perky. She leans toward me slightly, but her attitude seems more conspiratorial than concerned.

Realizing that she's not talking about church but about feeling like she doesn't measure up to the rest of the working girls, you can't quite stifle a little laugh. You're thinking about the many desperate, whispered confessions you've heard from Rose and other women through the years, and about the fact that most of them congregate here at Johnny's to drink and toke a bit before they can face another night on the stroll. Six or seven hours split between shivering on the corner and pretending to be pleased with the dangerous attentions of morons and misogynists. Then home to the gentle soul who holds the kids to make sure it keeps happening night after night.

"How long have you been working?" you ask, thinking that at her age and if she's typical, she'll have been "in the trade" for more than half her life.

"Just two years!" she says. "My mom's a minister"—she tells you the denomination—"I've never done this kind of thing before in my life! I'm thirty-five. That's pretty late to start, huh?"

It is indeed. You ask her what happened, how she ended up here.

"Well, I have a psychiatric condition," she says in the way you might tell someone you have a birthmark behind your knee. "I'm fine when I take my meds, but I got partying a little too much a few years ago and stopped taking them, and then things *really* fell apart, and then"—a tiny sigh, the first overt indication of any sort of distress—"and then I sort of ended up here."

She takes a careful sip from her drink, barely touching the straw so as to maintain the perfect red paint job on her lips.

"I'm fine now, though," she says, perky again. "At least, I'm back on my meds. I still feel like I'm running hard to keep up, but I keep slipping further back. These girls"—a glance at the women chattering nearby, the merest pucker of frown between her eyebrows—"they just seem to cruise along."

"We're all pretty much in the same boat, you know," is what you say to her. "Half the women in this place have told me in different ways that they feel just like you do. The wheels keep falling off in my own life, and I keep screwing up in the same ways, over and over."

"Really?" she asks, eager to believe it.

"Sure. We're all of us just keeping the most attractive cover we can on the mess underneath."

Her jaw drops briefly. We sit silent for a minute.

"Really?" she asks again.

"Uh-huh."

Pause. "Well, thank you for telling me that." She's pondering this revelation. You can almost see it sinking in: it's not just *me*... She looks down at the tabletop, not seeing the detritus of Coke cans, lipstick-rimmed Styrofoam cups, and empty french-fries containers.

"Thanks!" she says again, looking up. And flashes a perfect white smile.

A couple of weeks later, you see her posed on her patch of the street with another girl. She thanks you for the message you left about the church near where she's living—Jack, an old friend with years of street experience is an associate pastor there, and it just happened to be the same denomination as her mother's.

"I haven't actually gone yet," she says, watching your eyes carefully. "I'm still, you know, down *here*, so…"

She leaves it hanging, needing to know how you'll react. Wanting to know how it *really* is.

"It's okay," you say. "Jack's been this whole route" (gesturing around the street) "and he knows where you're coming from. Call him! He'll give you a ride."

Now you're looking her right in the eyes, because you know this next is what she's really waiting for: "And besides, the people in that church are all in the same boat as you and me. They're just trying to keep the most attractive cover they can on the mess underneath."

She lights up that smile and actually laughs. You're pretty sure she will make that call sooner or later.

The Hope of Redemption

Rose again, but a couple of years later, and on a cool spring night. The hair is a little shorter now and a different color. But for a kind of tightness around those wonderful hazel eyes, everything else initially seems much the same. She's standing less than thirty yards from the spot where she told you about laying herself down for her boys and confessed that God had been speaking to her.

She's more extravagant in her movements, a little wilder, a little less earth-motherly. You realize with a sinking heart that, as has become the pattern over the past year or so, she's been drinking or toking, or both. It seems now to be the only way she can face another night. Despite the manic activity, or maybe because of it, she radiates the weariness she began to speak of so long ago. Her weariness grabs your own heart, grants you a momentary flash of insight into the staggering emotional cost of doing what she does, and it seems to numb your soul. In this moment, you can hardly fathom how she survives.

You had been talking about the usual stuff—kids, weather (*This* is supposed to be spring? Whatever happened to global warming?)—but the impact of her weariness has caused you to lose the thread. You realize with a start that she is now talking about the future, not usually a popular topic. And she is speaking with some animation, not just a dreamy vagueness. She has a plan! A plan for a future and a hope, a plan to take these bitter years of street exile and turn them into something good.

She has applied to George Brown College, she says—and she's been accepted! She whirls around, hands reaching high above her head, hooting with laughter. What program? Community Worker! She's going to become a community worker! At this point, who knows how she'll manage moneywise. Paying the bills is not something she has entirely worked out yet. But someday, she'll be a community worker, and she'll spend her time counseling women in prison or women who've been assaulted.

Some of the other women nearby laugh and tease her: What does she know about women in prison? What kind of counseling will she be able to offer? They know that the only novelty there will be supplied by her being on the other side of the bars.

But it's all good natured, and Rose is laughing when she responds, "I been schoolin' you girls for years!"

And it's true. She's taught many of them how to stay relatively safe out here, how to watch out for one another, how to present themselves, and how to take care of business. She's been kind of a den mother. The other women go to her when they have problems, and they gather around her when one of their number goes down. She has offered words of comfort and encouragement to you, too.

You remind her of this. She looks at you, glances back at the women ten or fifteen feet way, and drops her voice.

God still talks to her, she tells you. She wonders if someday she might actually become a preacher—she's not really interested much in the actual preaching part, it's more looking after people; *preacher* is just the term that comes to mind. Rose seems pretty serious about all this, and a little puzzled. The pieces of that particular picture don't quite fit together just yet, but God keeps talking to her. And he really does like her, she's sure of that. Wouldn't that be something, though? To take all these years out here and get to use them to help other weary women find rest? Wouldn't that be something?

It is a continual surprise that God is willing to pour his glory ("the glory of God in the face of Christ") into a dusty, cracked— broken!—jar of clay like me.[6] It's just as surprising when I see that glory leaking out through somebody else's cracks. It's so surprising that it's easy to miss, easy to dispense with the ludicrous and faintly blasphemous notion that Jesus might be right here, right now. Seeing is not necessarily believing. Sometimes it's believing that allows me to see.

After all these years, it still requires of me a disciplined choosing to act or receive if I am to be the Christ or recognize him. Being present, abandoning power, picking up my cross—it's only by the deliberate choice to act in ways such as these that I can offer myself to others as the presence of Jesus. Only by choosing to be still can I see the hidden Jesus, experience the power of utterly abandoning myself into his arms, and receive resurrection life offered into my own motionless hands.

By no amount of effort can I save or regenerate myself. This is the work of God alone. But he still insists that *I* choose—he will not choose for me. Day by day, I am choosing, looking for Jesus's presence in myself and in others. I have come to expect that I will see him, but somehow, it's still always a surprise when he shows up. Now I see him momentarily in reflected images: distorted, fractured, obscured. I can hardly wait to see him face to face.

Notes

PROLOGUE: NEIL'S STORY

1. Matthew 25:36,40.
2. See Luke 24:13-33.
3. Philippians 2:5, KJV.
4. Henri Nouwen, *Making All Things New* (San Francisco: Harper, 1981), 68.

BEING PRESENT

1. Isaiah 1:5-6, NASB.
2. See Hebrews 2:14-15

SEEING: BEHOLDING THE HIDDEN JESUS

1. Isaiah 53:2.
2. Isaiah 52:14.
3. John 1:29, NASB.
4. Hosea 2:13.
5. Hosea 2:14.

BEING: THE ABANDONMENT OF POWER

1. See Ephesians 1:18-20.

SEEING: THE POWER OF ABANDONMENT

1. Ephesians 1:19-20.

2. Ephesians 1:7.

3. See John 13–17.

Being: Picking Up My Cross

1. See Mark 8:31-38 (Greg's paraphrase).

2. Ephesians 4:15, NASB.

3. Ephesians 4:13, NASB.

Seeing: Receiving the Gift of Life

1. John 11:25-26.

2. John 15:11; 16:24.

3. Matthew 25:21,23, NASB.

4. John 15:9.

5. Luke 14:17, KJV.

Epilogue: The Surprise of Brokenness

1. Hebrews 2:8-9.

2. See Hebrews 2:11.

3. Hebrews 5:7-8.

4. See Colossians 1:10-12.

5. See 1 Corinthians 3:11-13.

6. See 2 Corinthians 4:6-7.

About the Author

Greg Paul is the founder and executive director of Sanctuary Ministries of Toronto and pastor of the Sanctuary community. In addition to maintaining and perpetuating the vision for Sanctuary, Greg's role includes pastoral care, counseling and leadership, organizational partnerships, fund-raising, and representing Sanctuary to the public.

A former carpenter, Greg has been involved in inner-city ministry for over twenty-five years. His passionate commitment to the people on the street grew out of his fascination with the city and a strong interest in the issues of the street. Partnering with other organizations, Greg has developed the vision of building a community in which he and his family, as well as other staff and volunteers, live, work, and share the experiences of the people they are trying to help.

Greg is the lead vocalist and keyboardist for Red Rain, the band that planted the seed for Sanctuary in the mid-1980s. Red Rain has performed in bars, universities, jails, and a variety of other venues, as well as releasing three CDs.

Greg and his wife, Karen, were commended to work in the Toronto city core by Richvale Bible Church in March 1992. Greg and Karen have four children: Caleb, Jesse, Rachel, and Kelly.

About Sanctuary Ministries of Toronto

The essence of Sanctuary is that we intend to be a healthy, welcoming community centered on Jesus Christ. We make it a priority to welcome people who have, for the most part, known only rejection and abuse. Our core community includes:

- people who are homeless and people who run their own businesses
- middle-aged, middle-class people and squeegee kids
- university students and hardened street people

Sharing our lives and our resources, we reach out to a downtown neighborhood plagued with homelessness, drugs, prostitution, unemployment, and AIDS. We offer dignity, support, and direction to people who want to reclaim healthy, meaningful lives. Through drop-ins, street outreach, and one-to-one relationships, we offer food, clothing, and an invitation to deeper relationship. Our staff helps individuals access welfare, housing, legal counsel, medical care, therapy, or drug rehabilitation. Our health clinic provides care for soul and body to many who find it too difficult to access health care elsewhere. We've begun an employment-training initiative to help people reclaim their dignity and personal purpose through fulfilling work, and a pilot program aimed at creating real homes, instead of mere housing, for people who may never before have experienced a healthy home (with all that implies of family fellowship and security).

Perhaps the most valuable thing we offer is simple friendship.

Our staff and programs are funded almost entirely by donations, for which we issue receipts for income tax purposes. If you're interested in learning more about Sanctuary or in partnering with us, feel free to contact us:

Sanctuary
25 Charles Street East
Toronto, ON
Canada MRY 1R9

Telephone: 416-922-0628
E-mail: info@sanctuaryministries.on.ca
Web site: www.sanctuaryministries.on.ca